MW00514283

Recipes and Reminiscing

A Collection of Over 500 of the
Best Amish and Mennonite Recipes

Masthof Press
219 Mill Road
Morgantown, PA 19543-9516

Recipes and Reminiscing

Copyright © 2005

Illustrated by
Julie Stauffer Martin, Ephrata, Pa.

Library of Congress Number: 2005937657
International Standard Book Number: 1-932864-32-6

Published 2006 by
Masthof Press
219 Mill Road
Morgantown, PA 19543-9516

Reminisces are by various
contributors who would like
to remain anonymous.

Table of Contents

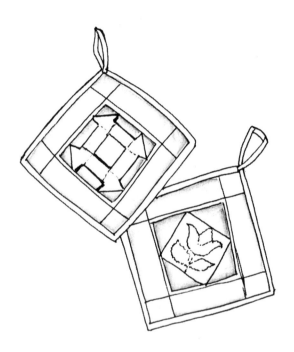

Breakfast Specials and Muffins

Childhood Memories

I had a pet rooster whose crowing on the back fence awoke me every morning. Mother would be in the kitchen cutting slices of cornmeal mush for the big black iron frying pan on the range. She would tell me (in a whisper so the younger ones wouldn't awaken right away) to hurry out to bring the cow in for milking. Then she would turn the burner of the gas stove on low, and go out to the barn to help with the chores before breakfast.

Fetching the cow was a delightful thing in the springtime, when the beauties of nature were reawakening. Almost every time I brought in bouquets of wildflowers or blossoms to put in a jar of water on the middle of the table.

I remember how delighted I was when I discovered that our horse, Beauty, had a cute little colt down in the meadow. It was so much fun to be the first to discover it.

When the chores were all done, and the little ones up and dressed, we all sat at our places around the big kitchen table. After Bible reading and saying a silent table grace, the food was passed around. Besides the heaping platter of fried mush, there were dozens of eggs fried sunny-side-up, a big kettle of oatmeal cooked with raisins, and a pitcher of steaming meadow tea or hot chocolate in winter. We always had pie for breakfast, too. Usually shoe-fly or other crumb pies and sometimes pumpkin or custard pies. Nowadays this would be considered too rich for breakfast, but we worked and played hard and none of us was fat.

In those days we had never heard of breakfast casseroles, which are so handy because they can be mixed the evening before, refrigerated, and baked in the morning. Breakfast was an important meal for us, because by the time the chores were finished, over 12 hours had passed since suppertime and we were all very hungry. After the meal was over we lingered at the table to discuss our work and plans for the day. My job was washing the breakfast dishes, including the big black frying pan, which I detested. Mother had to remind me more than once how thankful we should be to have plenty to eat and dirty dishes to wash.

Easy Breakfast Casserole

6 eggs
2 c. milk
1 tsp. salt
½ tsp. dry mustard
1 c. sharp cheese

3 slices bread, cubed
1 lb. pork sausage, crumbled,
  fried, and drained
corn flake crumbs (for topping, if desired)
¼ tsp. pepper

Beat eggs with milk, salt and mustard. Grease a 9" x 13" baking dish. Layer bread cubes, sausage, and cheese. Pour egg mixture over all and refrigerate overnight. Add corn flake crumbs, if desired, and bake at 350° for 40-45 min.

Egg and Cheese Casserole

4 slices bread (any kind)
1 lb. bulk or link sausage
2 c. milk
1 c. grated sharp
  cheddar cheese

6 eggs
1 tsp. mustard
1 tsp. salt
dash pepper

Tear bread in bits. Place in greased 13" x 9" x 2" baking dish. Brown bulk or link sausage; drain. (Cut link in slices.) Spoon sausage over bread. Sprinkle with grated cheddar cheese. Beat eggs, milk, salt and pepper. Pour over mixture in baking dish. Bake at 350° for 25 or 30 min. Serve with toast and applesauce. Serves 6-8.

Bacon Casserole

2-3 slices bread
1 c. sharp grated cheese
6 beaten eggs
½ tsp. salt

1 lb. bacon, fried and crumbled
2 c. milk
½ tsp. dry mustard

Break bread into sm. pieces; place in greased casserole. Fry bacon, drain. Spread over bread. Add cheese to beaten eggs, milk, salt and dry mustard. Pour over bread and bacon. Refrigerate overnight or all day. Bake 1 hr. at 350°. Halve recipe for 3-4 persons.

Ham and Egg Casserole

1 lb. cubed ham	2½ c. milk
½ lb. cheddar cheese	4 eggs
14 slices bread,	½ tsp. mustard
crusts removed	1 tsp. minced onion

Layer bread, cheese and ham upon one another in a 13" x 9" Pyrex dish. Mix remaining ingredients and pour over layers; let stand in refrigerator overnight. Bake at 350° for 1 hr.

Egg and Bacon Bake

6 slices bacon	5 hard cooked eggs, sliced
2 med. onions, sliced	2 c. shredded cheese (optional)
1 can cream of	dash of salt and pepper
mushroom soup	English muffins, split and toasted
¼ c. milk	

Heat oven to 350°. Fry bacon until crisp, remove from skillet. Drain fat, reserving 2 T. and sauté onions in bacon fat. Stir in soup, milk, cheese and seasonings. Pour into 10" x 6" baking dish; top with crumbled bacon. Bake 20 min. Serve over split, toasted muffins or toasted bread. Serves 6 to 8.

Bisquick Ham Bake

1½ c. Bisquick biscuit mix	Parsley flakes and pepper
12 thin slices cooked ham	1 tsp. instant minced onion
6 eggs	¼ c. plus 2 T. cold water

Mix Bisquick, water and onion. Press in bottom and sides of 6 greased custard cups Line each with 2 slices ham. Break egg into each cup. Sprinkle with pepper and parsley. Bake on lowest rack at 400°, 15 to 18 min.

Bacon 'N Egg Pizza

1 - 8 oz. can refrigerated	5 slices crisp bacon, crumbled
biscuits or make	1 tsp. chopped chives or onion
your own dough	1 c. shredded cheddar cheese
Dash of salt	3 eggs, beaten
1 T. milk	

Flatten biscuits on pizza pan. Combine eggs, milk and salt. Pour onto biscuit shell. Sprinkle with bacon, chives and cheese. Bake at 350° for 20 min. Top with crisp bacon slices if desired.

Potato Egg Brunch

4 strips bacon, fried	1 c. milk
4 c. diced, cooked potatoes	Salt and pepper
3 hard-boiled eggs, chopped	Minced onion
1 can cream of chicken soup	½ c. shredded cheese

Crumble fried bacon. Layer potatoes, bacon and eggs in casserole. Blend soup, milk, onion, salt and pepper. Pour over top. Sprinkle with cheese. Bake at 350° for 30 min.

Eggs in Hot Sauce

6 hard-boiled eggs	Dash of pepper
2 T. butter	2 c. milk
2 T. flour	6 to 8 slices toast
1 tsp. salt	

Peel and chop eggs. Melt butter in saucepan. Add flour and seasoning. Stir until well blended. Add milk, stirring constantly. Cook until smooth. Add eggs to hot sauce. Serve on toast.

Mushroom Egg Bake

5 hard-cooked eggs	¼ tsp. salt
1 - 3 oz. can sliced	¼ tsp. onion salt
mushrooms	½ c. minced celery
½ c. milk	½ c. packaged poultry stuffing
3 T. margarine	½ c. grated cheddar cheese
2 T. flour	

Drain juice from mushrooms into measuring cup, adding milk to make 1 c. Heat mushrooms in 1 T. margarine. Slice eggs into casserole and sprinkle with mushrooms. Add remaining butter to saucepan. Melt and stir in flour, salt and then milk mixture. Cook until thickened. Add celery and pour over eggs. Mix cheese and stuffing; sprinkle over top. Bake in a 375° oven for about 20 min.

Cottage Cheese Casserole

1 c. biscuit mix (Bisquick)	1 tsp. dried parsley flakes or
1½ c. cottage cheese	1 T. fresh parsley
½ lb. grated cheddar	¼ tsp. salt
cheese	6 eggs, lightly beaten
1 tsp. dried onion or	1 c. milk
2 tsp. fresh onion	¾ c. butter

Mix ingredients in order given, except butter. Melt butter in 13" x 9" x 2" baking dish. Pour cheese-egg mixture, spreading evenly. Bake at 350° about 40 min.

Cheddar Cheese Bake

1 lb. sausage	1 can mushroom soup
12 eggs, well beaten	½ c. milk
¼ lb. cheddar cheese, grated	

In skillet, brown sausage, stirring until crumbly. Drain and remove from skillet. Scramble eggs in a sm. amount of pan drippings until partially set. Mix together soup and milk in a separate bowl. In a 1½ qt. rectangular casserole dish, layer sausage and eggs. Top with soup mixture and cheese. Bake at 350° until cheese is melted. Makes 8 servings.

Creamed Bacon Casserole

6 bacon slices	5 hard-cooked eggs, sliced
2 med. onions, sliced	2 c. (8 oz.) shredded cheddar cheese
1 can condensed cream of	Dash of salt and pepper
mushroom soup	English muffins, split, toasted
¼ c. milk	

Heat oven to 350°. Fry bacon until crisp; remove from skillet. Drain fat, reserving 2 T. Sauté onion in bacon fat. Stir in soup, milk, eggs, cheese and seasonings. Pour into 6" x 10" baking dish. Top with crumbled bacon. Bake at 350° for 20 min. Serve over muffin halves. Makes 6 to 8 servings.

Home—the place where our stomachs
get 3 square meals a day, and our hearts a thousand.

Crouton Brunch

4 c. croutons	¾ tsp. dry mustard
2 c. cheddar cheese, grated	2½ c. milk
1 lb. sausage	1 can cream of mushroom soup
½ c. milk	4 eggs

Spread croutons in a 9" x 13" dish. Brown and drain sausage. Put cheese and sausage over croutons. Beat eggs; add 2½ c. milk and mustard. Pour over all; refrigerate overnight. Dilute soup with remaining milk and add before baking. Bake 1½ hr. at 350°.

Ham, Egg and Cheese Bake

2 c. shredded ham	2 c. milk
4 slices bread	1 tsp. dry mustard (optional)
1 c. sharp grated cheese	1 tsp. salt
6 eggs	Dash of pepper

Tear bread and place in greased 13" x 9" x 2" baking dish. Spoon ham over bread. Sprinkle with cheese. Beat eggs, milk, mustard, salt and pepper. Pour mixture over bread in baking dish. Let stand in refrigerator overnight. Bake in preheated oven at 350° for 30-40 min. Makes 6-8 servings. May be halved easily.

Breakfast Cheeseburger Pie

1 lb. hamburger	1 c. shredded cheddar cheese
1½ c. chopped onions	1½ c. milk
½ tsp. salt	¾ c. Bisquick
¼ tsp. pepper	3 eggs

Heat oven to 400°. Lightly grease a 10" pie plate. Cook and stir beef and onions until brown; drain. Stir in salt and pepper. Spread beef mixture in pie plate; sprinkle with cheese. Beat remaining ingredients until smooth. Pour over meat and cheese in pie plate. Bake until golden brown and knife inserted in center comes out clean, about 30 min. Let stand 5 min.

English Muffin Melt

2 eggs
1 slice cheese

1 thin slice ham
1 slice bread or English muffin

Scramble eggs and fry lightly. Top with cheese. Put ham on muffin and eggs on top. Cover till ready to serve so cheese melts. Serves 1.

Wheat Germ Pancakes

1 c. flour
½ c. wheat flour
½ tsp. salt (scant)
¼ c. wheat germ or bran

2 tsp. soda (scant)
Approx. 2 c. thick sour milk,
   more if needed

Combine flour, salt and soda. Add milk and wheat germ, and then mix. Fry in lots of butter or margarine. Sometimes I add more wheat germ or bran.

Whole Wheat Pancakes

2 c. whole wheat flour
½ tsp. salt
1 T. melted butter
3 T. sugar

4 tsp. baking powder
1½ c. milk
2 eggs beaten

Sift together dry ingredients, add milk, butter and eggs. Beat until blended. Bake on slightly greased hot griddle.

Katie's Cornmeal Pancakes

1 c. flour
1 c. cornmeal
1 T. baking powder
1 tsp. salt

1¾ c. milk
2 eggs, slightly beaten
2 T. vegetable oil

Combine dry ingredients. In mixing bowl, combine milk with beaten eggs; add dry ingredients. Stir only until lumps disappear. Add vegetable oil. Makes fifteen 4" pancakes.

Honey Pancakes

2 beaten eggs	2 c. sour milk (Add 2 T. vinegar
2 tsp. sugar	if sweet milk is used)
2 tsp. baking powder	2½ c. flour
2 T. honey	4 T. melted butter or oil
1 tsp. salt	

Beat eggs till light. Add milk and honey. Sift flour with baking powder, salt and sugar. Beat flour mixture into egg mixture. Add melted butter. Beat until smooth.

Plain Pancakes

2 well beaten eggs	5 T. salad oil or melted butter
2 c. milk	3 tsp. baking powder
½ c. sugar	1 tsp. salt
2¼ c. flour	

Stir together sugar, salt, flour and baking powder. Add eggs, oil or butter, and milk.

Potato Pancakes

2 c. grated raw potatoes	2 T. milk
4 T. flour	1 tsp. baking powder
1 egg beaten	2 T. butter
1 tsp. salt	

Mix all together. Drop by spoonfuls into skillet, fry in mixed butter and lard until brown and crispy.

Zucchini Pancakes

Approx. 2 sm. fresh	2 eggs
zucchini squash	½ c. milk
2 c. pancake mix	

Grate squash. Put all ingredients, except milk, into a bowl. Beat, gradually adding milk. You may need more or less milk. Eat with butter and honey or syrup. Yields 12 to 14 pancakes.

Pancake Syrup

1 c. sugar   2 c. water

Bring to boil; add 1 level T. cornstarch. Mix with a little water, bring to a full rolling boil, add 1 tsp. maple flavor and ½ tsp. vanilla.

Cinnamon Pancakes

2 beaten eggs   2 c. sour milk
1 tsp. soda   2¼ c. flour
2 tsp. baking powder   1 tsp. salt
4 T. melted butter   2 T. sugar
½ tsp. cinnamon

(If sweet milk is used, omit the soda and increase baking powder to 3 tsp.)

Beat eggs until fluffy. Add milk. Sift flour, baking powder, cinnamon, soda, salt and sugar. Beat flour mixture into egg mixture. Mix well. Add melted butter and beat until smooth.

Make-Ahead Pancake Mix

Mix:
10 c. flour   3 T. soda
3 T. salt   5 heaping T. baking powder
¼ c. sugar   2 c. oatmeal (quick)
3 c. whole wheat flour   3 c. crushed corn flakes

Mix thoroughly and store until used.

To make batter, use:
1 c. mix   1 c. milk
1 egg   1 T. shortening

Lightest Ever Pancakes

2 c. sifted flour   1 tsp. soda
3 T. sugar   ¾ tsp. salt
2 eggs, well beaten   ¼ c. vinegar
1¾ c. sweet milk   ¼ c. shortening (melted)

Sift flour, baking soda, sugar and salt together. Combine eggs, vinegar, milk and shortening and mix well. Add to dry ingredients and stir only until smooth. Pour into hot frying pan. When edge has formed a crust, turn.

Maple Syrup

4 c. brown sugar   ½ c. molasses
2 c. water   2 tsp. maple flavoring

Bring the sugar, water and molasses to a boil. Remove from heat and add maple flavoring.

Amish Granola

8 c. oatmeal   4 c. wheat germ
2 c. bran   1½ c. coconut
1 c. nuts or sunflower seeds

Pour 1 c. honey and 1 c. oil over ingredients. Bake 1 hr. at 200-225°, stirring often.

Cinnamon Raisin Granola

12 c. rolled oats   6 c. wheat germ
1 c. brown sugar or   3 c. coconuts and 3 c. nuts
   1 c. honey mixed   1½ c. raisins
   with 1 c. veg. oil   1½ tsp. salt
   or melted oleo or   1½ tsp. cinnamon
   butter

Mix all together and pour in cake pans. Toast in oven until coconut turns brown. Stir often while toasting at 325°.

Tasty Granola

12 c. rolled oats   5 c. wheat germ
1 c. melted shortening   add a little cinnamon
5 c. coconut   2 c. brown sugar, more or less
1 tsp. salt   2 c. sunflower seeds

Mix all together and brown lightly in oven. Cool and store in airtight container. Serve with milk and honey.

Breakfast Delight

2 c. rolled oats   1 c. brown sugar
1 tsp. salt   ½ c. coconut
2 c. wheat flour   1 tsp. soda
½ c. butter

Mix into crumbs; then put on cookie sheet and roast in oven at 400°.

Crunchy Cereal

14 c. oatmeal   6 c. coconut
4 c. wheat germ   3 c. brown sugar
1 c. butter   pinch of salt
2 c. nuts

Mix dry things together before adding butter. Toast in oven. Makes 2 gal.

Grandma's Granola

16 c. quick oatmeal   2 tsp. cinnamon
2 c. coconut   2 tsp. salt
2 c. wheat germ   2 c. vegetable oil or melted margarine
4 c. brown sugar   2 tsp. vanilla

Mix dry ingredients in a bowl. Add vanilla to oil and add to dry ingredients. Mix well. Bake at 250° until slightly browned, stirring occasionally.

Sesame Granola

15 c. oatmeal   12 T. sesame seeds
3 c. wheat germ   3 c. brown sugar
3 c. sunflower seeds   1½ c. concentrated orange juice
3 c. nuts   2 c. vegetable oil
1 T. salt   1 T. vanilla
3 c. coconut

Mix all the dry ingredients together. Mix concentrate, oil and vanilla together, then add to the dry ingredients. Bake at 250° until crisp, stirring occasionally.

Flaxseed Granola

10 c. oatmeal	1¾ c. vegetable oil or melted butter
4 c. whole wheat flour	1 c. coconut
2 c. white flour	2 c. brown sugar
2 tsp. salt	1 c. sunflower seeds or nuts
½ c. ground flaxseed	

Mix all ingredients together in large bowl. Toast in oven at low to med. heat till coconut turns brown. Stir occasionally. Best when eaten with fresh strawberries or other fruit.

Best Grape Nuts

8 lb. whole wheat flour	5 lb. brown sugar
1¼ tsp. salt	2 T. soda
2 T. vanilla	2 T. maple
¾ lb. oleo (melted)	2½ qt. buttermilk or sour milk

Put together in order given, adding flour last. Put in greased cake pans and bake 30-40 min. till done in 350° oven. Cool overnight. Put through shredder and bake them again in a slow oven until nice and brown. Seal in tight jars to keep.

Old-fashioned Grape Nuts

7 c. wheat flour	3 c. brown sugar
4 c. sour milk	2 tsp. soda
2 tsp. salt	½ c. melted oleo
2 tsp. vanilla	2 tsp. maple flavoring

Bake as a loaf cake. Crumble and toast. Instead of 4 c. sour milk, use part cream or buttermilk.

Plain Muffins

1¾ c. flour	½ tsp. salt
¾ c. milk	⅓ c. butter or oleo
1 egg	3 tsp. baking powder
¼ c. sugar	

Mix ingredients as listed and bake in muffin tins at 400°.

Basic Grape Nuts

3 qt. brown sugar
    (slightly packed)
1¼ T. salt
2 T. vanilla
2½ qt. buttermilk

5 qt. whole wheat flour
2 T. soda
1½ tsp. maple flavor
¾ lb. oleo

Put dry ingredients in bowl except soda which should be added to milk. Last add melted oleo and flavor. Dough should be fairly thick. Bake at 350°. Makes about 15 lb.

Millie's Waffles

3 c. sifted flour
¾ tsp. salt
3 egg yolks, beaten
3 egg whites
    stiffly beaten, add last
To bake in waffle iron.

3½ tsp. baking powder
¾ c. Crisco
2 c. milk

Apple Muffins

3½ c. all-purpose flour
3 c. peeled, finely
    chopped apples
2 c. sugar
1 tsp. salt

1 tsp. baking soda
1 tsp. cinnamon
1½ c. vegetable oil
½ c. chopped nuts, toasted
1 tsp. vanilla

Preheat oven to 350°. Grease and flour muffin pans. Combine flour, apples, sugar, salt, soda and cinnamon in large bowl. Stir in oil, nuts and vanilla. Divide batter among muffin pans, filling about ½-⅔ full. Bake until toothpick inserted in center comes out clean, about 30 min.

Raisin Bran Muffins

1 - 15 oz. box Raisin Bran
1 c. melted butter
1 qt. buttermilk
5 c. flour

5 tsp. soda
3 c. sugar
4 beaten eggs
2 tsp. salt

Mix all together and use as needed. Place in muffin tins (greased) and bake at 400° for 20 min. Store batter in airtight container. Will store up to 4 weeks.

Raisin Oatmeal Muffins

¾ c. flour
2 tsp. baking powder
¾ tsp. salt
⅓ c. sugar
1 c. rolled oats

1 c. dark, seedless raisins
2 eggs, slightly beaten
½ c. milk
¼ c. cooking oil

Sift flour with baking powder, salt and sugar into bowl; stir in oats and raisins. Combine eggs, milk and oil. Add to flour mixture; mix thoroughly with fork just until dry ingredients are moistened. Fill greased muffin cups ⅔ full. Bake at 400° about 20 min. Makes 12 muffins.

Whole Wheat Muffins

2 T. butter or oleo, softened
2 eggs
3 T. honey
½ c. all-purpose flour
1½ c. whole wheat flour

1 tsp. baking powder
1 tsp. soda
1 tsp. salt
1 c. buttermilk

Combine butter and eggs, beating well; stir in honey. Combine dry ingredients; add to butter mixture alternately with buttermilk, beating well after each addition. Spoon into well-greased muffin pans. Bake at 350° for 20 min. Yields 1 dozen. Note: One T. lemon juice or vinegar added to 1 c. sweet milk equals 1 c. buttermilk.

Susie's Muffins

1 c. white flour
½ c. brown sugar
1 egg
½ tsp. soda

1 c. graham flour
½ c. shortening
1 tsp. baking powder
½ tsp. salt

Mix dry ingredients, then add milk, beaten eggs, melted shortening and the rest of ingredients. Mix quickly, pour in greased muffin tins and bake 20 min. in 400° oven or until done. Eat with fruit and milk, like shortcake.

Honey Muffins

¼ c. brown sugar	¼ c. honey
2 packages sweetener	2 eggs
½ c. oleo	

Mix and beat well and add:

1 c. plain yogurt	1 c. bran
1 c. oatmeal	½ c. flour
1 tsp. baking soda	¾ c. raisins
1 tsp. cinnamon	

Bake in greased muffin tins 15-20 min. at 400° or until done.

Wonder Muffins

1 c. flour	2½ c. bran flakes
⅓ c. brown sugar	1 c. milk
1 T. baking powder	1 egg
½ tsp. salt	⅓ c. vegetable oil

Mix flour with sugar, baking powder and salt. Combine cereal and milk in bowl and let stand for 3 min.; stir well. Add egg and oil; blend well. Add flour mixture to cereal mixture (batter will be thick). Spoon into greased muffin pans. Bake at 400° for 25 min. or until golden brown. Serve warm. Makes 12 muffins.

Cornmeal Raisin Muffins

1 c. cornmeal	4 tsp. baking powder
1 c. flour	1 c. milk
¼ c. sugar	2 eggs
1 tsp. salt	4 T. melted butter
½ c. raisins	

Mix dry ingredients together. Beat together remaining ingredients; add to flour mixture, stirring just enough to moisten. Bake at 400° approximately 20 min. Makes 24.

Molasses Muffins

2 c. whole wheat flour
2 T. melted butter
2 c. buttermilk
2 T. honey
½ c. dark molasses

1¼ tsp. baking soda
1½ c. pure unprocessed bran
½ tsp. salt
1 egg

Combine flour, bran, honey, salt and soda. Mix well. Combine remaining ingredients and stir into dry ingredients, just enough to moisten. Spoon into well-greased muffin tins, filling them ⅔ full. Bake at 350° for 20 to 25 min. Makes 2 dozen muffins.

Cinnamon Muffins

1 c. flour
1 c. whole wheat flour
4 tsp. baking powder
1 tsp. salt
½ tsp. cinnamon

1 egg
¾ c. milk
¼ c. brown sugar
4 T. melted shortening

Mix dry ingredients together. Beat remaining ingredients and add, stirring just enough to moisten. Bake at 400° for 20 to 25 min.

A godly woman sure should be
A Sarah to her Lord,
A Martha to her company
A Mary to the word.

A virtous woman is not one who sparkles with jewelry,
but with her love for her family.

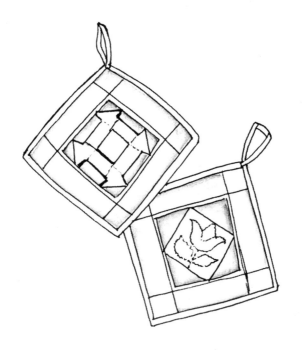

Breads, Rolls, and Doughnuts

Family Get-Togethers

We were a big, extended family, and the get-togethers were so much fun to us youngsters. Seeing all the cousins, aunts, uncles and grandparents once again was a treat in itself, not to mention all the scrumptious covered dishes that were brought. After a huge dinner, we cousins would run off to play kickball, tag, or prisoners base, and believe it or not, in a few hours we'd be famished again.

Grandma always made her specialty—a big kettleful of chicken potpie. The aunts brought various tasty casseroles, luscious desserts and baked goodies. In the afternoon there was a candy scramble for the children, sponsored by Aunt Naomi. No get-together would have been complete without that! We were each given a small bag, and what fun we had, shrieking and dashing here and there trying to fill them. I always hoarded my candy carefully, eating only 2 pieces each day so that it would last several weeks. My younger brother ate most of his in a few days' time, then begged me for some of mine. I was afraid he would sneak some, so I hid my stash away carefully, changing the hiding place several times. One time I got an unexpected chance to go to my cousin's place for a several days' stay, and when I got back home I couldn't remember where I had hid my candy! I hunted high and low, but it had disappeared. That fall when Mother was housecleaning, she found my bag of candy under the blanket chest, far back near the wall. It was no longer edible, and how I wished I'd have allowed my brother to have it instead, for I had felt stingy. The next time I generously shared with him, which gave me a much better feeling inside.

Betsy's Whole Wheat Bread

3 T. yeast
3 tsp. sugar
4½ T. maple syrup
    or molasses
3 tsp. salt

1½ c. warm water
3 c. potato water
6 T. sugar
9 c. whole wheat flour
2½ c. melted butter

Dissolve yeast in warm water and 3 tsp. sugar. Mix potato water, maple syrup, sugar and salt. Add yeast and whole wheat flour. Add melted butter. Mix well and let stand 12 min., then mix enough white bread flour to make a soft but not sticky dough. Let rise to double. Punch down and let rise again. When double in bulk, shape into loaves and let rise 1 hr. Bake at 350° for 30-35 min.

Buttermilk Bread

Heat 6 c. buttermilk or fresh milk
Add 3 T. molasses (or natural brown sugar)

3 T. honey
2 T. salt (less can be used)

¾ c. soy oil or veg. oil
3 c. warm water

Soak 3 T. of yeast in the warm water, cool boiled milk to lukewarm. Add all ingredients together after yeast has soaked 15 min. Stir in a few c. of flour at a time, beating and stirring till all the flour is stirred in (25 c. more or less). Knead good to a sponge-shape and put into 6 greased pans. Let rise some (not double in size). Put in hot oven at 450° for 15 min. Lower heat to 300° for 45 min. or longer.

Honey Oatmeal Bread

3 c. boiling water
1 c. honey or ½ c. sugar
2 T. yeast
4 eggs
½ c. oil

2 c. oatmeal
2 T. salt
1 c. warm water
1-3 c. whole wheat flour
Bread flour to finish

Pour boiling water over oatmeal. Let stand ½ hr. Add honey (or sugar), oil and salt. Dissolve yeast in warm water. Add eggs. Combine the two mixtures. Add whole wheat flour. Finish with bread flour. Makes 4 loaves.

Easy White Bread

3 c. warm water	½ c. sugar
2 T. salt (scant)	⅓ c. corn oil
2 T. or 2 pkg. dry yeast	9 c. bread flour

Water should be very warm but not hot when tested on inside of wrist. Combine water, sugar, salt, yeast and oil. Let stand until yeast dissolved. Stir in 5 c. flour. Beat until smooth. Add remaining flour until dough can be handled. Turn out onto a greased surface and knead vigorously with both hands 5-10 min. Cover. Set in warm place to rise for 30 min. Then knead lightly. Let rise for 1 hr. then divide dough and put into greased pans. Let set for 30 min., then knead each loaf a few seconds. Repeat in about 30 min. Then prick each loaf deeply with a fork. Let rise until double in size or until light. Bake for 20-30 min. at 350-400°. Turn twice while baking. Grease top of loaf when removing from oven. Makes 3 loaves.

100% Rye Bread

Dissolve: 2 T. yeast in ¼ c. lukewarm water. Add 2 c. water, ⅓ c. vegetable oil, 2 T. salt, ¼ c. sugar. Have the above mixture lukewarm, and work in about 6 c. rye flour. Let rise until double, then work it down and let it rise again. Put in 2 loaves and bake at 350° for 45-50 min.

Favorite Bread

4 c. warm water	4 T. yeast
½ c. sugar	3 tsp. salt
½ c. oleo	12-14 c. flour

Measure warm water into bowl. Sprinkle in yeast and stir till dissolved. Add sugar, salt, oleo and 6 c. flour to make a soft dough; stir well. Then add the rest of the flour. Let rise 1 hr.; knead, then rise 1 hr.; knead again. Let rise another hr. and make into 4 loaves. Bake at 375° for 30 min. or until done.

Sadie's Oatmeal Bread

2½ c. boiling water	2 c. quick oats (uncooked)
½ c. honey or brown sugar	2 T. salt
¾ c. cooking oil	4 eggs
2 pkg. yeast	2 c. whole wheat flour or more

Dissolve yeast in ½ c. warm water with 1 tsp. brown sugar (unless you use instant yeast, then you don't need to dissolve it). Put boiling water in bowl, add oats, whole wheat flour, salt, cooking oil and honey. Cool to lukewarm. Add eggs, yeast and enough bread flour to finish. Knead twice. Makes 4 sm. loaves. Bake in 400° oven for 10 min. Reduce heat to 350° for another 25 min.

Garlic Bread

Mix:
1½ c. flour
2 pkg. yeast

Heat until just warm:
1 c. milk	2 T. sugar
2 tsp. garlic salt	½ c. warm water
2 T. butter	

Add to flour mixture.
Then add:
2 eggs	½ c. parmesan cheese
3½ c. flour	

Let rise till doubled. Work down. Let set 10 min. Shape into balls. Dip in melted butter and parmesan cheese. Let rise until double. Bake at 375° for 20-25 min.

Wilma's White Bread

1 T. or pkg. of dry yeast	¾ c. sugar
½ c. shortening	1 T. salt
Enough flour to knead	2 qt. warm water of milk or potato water may be added, and just that much less water

Soak yeast in a c. of warm water, mix in the rest of ingredients with warm liquid (not hot). Stir yeast in and enough flour, a little at a time, and knead good with plenty of grease until it gets elastic. Let rise in a greased bowl for 10-15 min. Punch down, let rise again for 10-15 min. Punch down, let rise till double in size; punch down and shape and divide into loaves. Makes 4 or 5 loaves depending on your size of pans. Let rise, then bake for 45 min. in 350° oven. Secret is in letting it rise and punching down every 10-15 min.

Glazed Bread

3 c. warm water	3 T. yeast
3 T. sugar	
Let set 10 min.	

Add:

¼ c. shortening (melted)	1 T. salt
5 c. bread flour	

Work in 3-4 more c. of flour. Let rise once. Work out in 3 long loaves. Place on cookie sheets. Slash with sharp knife. Let rise again.

Brush on top before baking:
1 egg beaten
1 T. water

Bake at 350° for 30 min.

Cornbread Loaf

1 c. cornmeal	1 c. flour
4 tsp. baking powder	½ tsp. salt
¼ c. sugar	1 egg
½ c. shortening (melted)	1 c. milk

Mix together in order given. Mix real good. Pour in greased 9" x 12" pan. Bake at 325° for ¾ hr.

Maple Oatmeal Bread

2½ c. boiling water	2 c. quick oatmeal
¾ c. cooking oil	2 c. whole wheat flour (or more)
1 c. maple or pancake	4 beaten eggs
syrup	2 pkg. dry yeast
2 T. salt	Enough white flour to knead

Dissolve yeast in 1 c. warm water. Pour boiling water over oatmeal and set aside to cool till lukewarm. Mix all ingredients and beat well, then add yeast, being sure everything is just warm before adding. Work in enough white flour (preferably unbleached) to make a nice spongy dough that is not sticky. Grease top and let rise; knead and let rise again. Bake at 400° for 10 min., lower heat to 350° for 25 to 30 min. A delicious nourishing bread. You may use as much wheat flour as you wish.

Health Bread

2 pkg. or cakes of yeast	1 c. dry milk solids
2 c. water	½ c. regular rolled oats
½ c. molasses	½ c. yellow cornmeal
4 egg yolks	½ c. wheat germ
2½ tsp. salt	1 c. rye flour or rye meal
⅓ c. corn oil	2 c. whole wheat flour
3 c. white flour	

Sprinkle dry yeast or crumble yeast cakes into warm water in large bowl, add molasses. Let stand for a few min., then stir until dissolved. Add egg yolks, salt, oil, dry milk, oats, cornmeal, and wheat germ. Beat until well mixed. Add rye flour, whole wheat flour and enough white flour to make stiff dough. Mix well. Brush lightly with oil, cover, and let rise till doubled. If punched down and allowed to rise again, this dough will have a finer texture, but is not necessary. Turn out onto floured pastry board or cloth, and knead gently. Shape into 2 loaves. Put in greased 9" x 5" x 3" loaf pans. Let rise until doubled. Bake in preheated 375° oven for 24 min. Reduce heat to 350° and bake about 20 min. longer.

Honey Wheat Bread

3½ c. boiling water	¾ c. cooking oil
1 c. honey, karo or molasses	3 pkg. dry yeast
2 T. salt	2 c. quick oatmeal
5 beaten eggs	6 c. wheat flour (or more)

Dissolve yeast in 1 c. warm water. Pour boiling water over oatmeal and set aside to cool till lukewarm. Mix all ingredients and beat well, then add yeast, being sure everything is just warm, before adding. Work in enough white flour (preferably unbleached) to make a nice spongy dough that is not sticky. Grease top and let rise. Knead and let rise again. Bake at 400° for 10 min. Lower heat to 350° for 25-30 min. A delicious nourishing bread. You may use as much wheat flour as you wish.

Boston Brown Bread

1 c. raisins, cooked in 2 c. water until puffy. Cool and mix in:

1 c. sugar	1 c. white flour
2 tsp. soda	1 tsp. shortening
¼ c. molasses	½ tsp. salt
½ tsp. vanilla	1 egg
1 c. whole wheat flour	½ c. chopped nuts

Grease 3 No. 2 size cans and fill ⅔ full of mixture. Bake 1 hr. at 350°. Cool slightly before removing from cans. Slice and serve with butter or cream cheese, as bread or as a dessert with coffee. A greased loaf pan or large juice can may be used instead of sm. cans.

Gypsy Bread

2 eggs	1½ c. oil
1 c. honey	4 T. salt
6 T. yeast in warm water	2 sticks oleo or butter, melted
3 c. milk heated to boiling point	

Add other ingredients and yeast, then add:

3 c. cold water	10 c. wheat flour
12 c. white flour	

Knead dough 15 min. Rise till double, then knead real good. Let rise again, then put in pans. Do not overrise in pans before baking. Bake at 375° for 30 min. Makes around 8-9 big loaves. It does not rise much in oven.

Norma's Whole Wheat Bread

1 stick margarine (melted)
Scald: 2⅔ c. milk then cool
Dissolve 2 T. dry yeast in 2 c. warm water

2 beaten eggs	1 scant c. sugar
2 tsp. salt	

Mix all the ingredients together. Add 5 c. whole wheat flour and white flour to finish.

Molasses Wheat Bread

½ c. vegetable oil
2 c. warm water
1½ c. oatmeal
6-8 c. flour

⅔ c. molasses (scant)
2 eggs
2 pkg. yeast

Mix in order given. Knead till smooth and elastic. Place in a greased bowl, let rise till double in bulk. Punch down. Let rise 10 min. Shape into loaves–2 lg. or 4 sm. Let rise until double in bulk and bake at 350° for 20-30 min.

Raisin Bread

6 c. lukewarm water
1 c. white sugar
6 T. dry yeast
2 heaping c. raisins

4 T. vegetable oil
6 tsp. salt
2 heaping T. cinnamon
12-14 c. bread flour

Proceed with flour as for white bread.

Swedish Rye Bread

2 pkg. active dry yeast
1 tsp. sugar
3 tsp. salt
9¼ c. white flour
½ c. white sugar
3 c. hot water

1½ c. rye flour
½ c. molasses
½ c. melted vegetable
　　shortening
½ c. warm water (110° or 115°)

Dissolve yeast in warm water. Stir in 1 tsp. sugar, set aside. In large mixing bowl mix rye flour with ½ c. sugar and salt. Add hot water gradually, mixing to a smooth paste. Gradually add melted shortening and molasses. Beat well. Add yeast mixture and white flour. When dough becomes too still to work with spoon, knead in remaining flour until dough is smooth and elastic. Place in warm area until double in bulk. Divide into 3 loaves and place in greased 9" x 5" x 3" pans. Let rise until double. Bake at 325° for 40 min. Remove from pans and rub tops and sides with melted shortening.

Single Loaf Bread

1 c. warm water
1 tsp. salt
1 T. sugar

1 tsp. lard or cooking oil
1 tsp. dry yeast
3 c. flour

Combine first five ingredients in order given. Let stand until yeast dissolves. Stir in flour, beat until smooth, add remaining flour. Work dough in bowl for 5-10 min. Let stand until double. Put in bread pan. Let stand for ½ hr. Knead and prick deeply with fork. Let stand till ready to bake. Bake in hot oven.

Zucchini Bread

3 eggs
2 c. sugar
1 c. vegetable oil
3 tsp. vanilla
3 c. flour
2 c. grated, raw,
    peeled zucchini

1 tsp. salt
1 tsp. baking soda
¼ tsp. baking powder
3 tsp. cinnamon
1 c. chopped walnuts

Grease and flour two 9" x 5" x 3" loaf pans. Beat eggs until light and fluffy in large mixing bowl. Add sugar, oil, zucchini and vanilla to eggs and mix well. Combine dry ingredients, add to zucchini mixture. Mix well; stir in nuts. Pour in pans and bake at 350° for 1 hr. Cool on racks. This freezes well.

Mary's Gingerbread

1 c. molasses
1 c. milk, sweet or sour
2 tsp. soda
1 tsp. ginger

½ c. lard
3 c. flour
1 tsp. cream of tartar

Good with the following sauce poured over each serving.

Sauce:
½ c. brown sugar

2 T. cornstarch

Add 1 c. boiling water slowly, add ½ c. raisins. Cook slowly 5 min., add 1 T. butter.

Angel Bread

5 c. flour	1 c. shortening
⅓ c. sugar	2 c. buttermilk
3 tsp. baking powder	1 tsp. soda
1 tsp. salt	2 pkg. dry yeast dissolved in
	½ c. warm water

Sift together dry ingredients. Cut shortening in flour mixture. Add buttermilk and yeast mixture; mix well. Add extra flour, if needed.

Cover and place in refrigerator. Remove and roll out what you need for a meal. Cut into biscuits and let stand ½ hr. or longer. Bake in hot oven (425°). Dough will keep 1 week.

Monkey Bread

5 cans biscuits	cinnamon
1 stick butter	sugar

Cut biscuits into quarters. Mix enough cinnamon and sugar to coat biscuits; put all in paper bag and shake. Place coated biscuits in a tube pan and pour melted butter over. Bake at 350° until done. Pull apart to eat.

Apple Dapple Bread

3 c. flour	1 tsp. soda
2 tsp. cinnamon	½ tsp. baking powder
½ tsp. salt	½ tsp. oil
2 c. sugar	2 eggs (beaten)
½ tsp. vanilla	3 c. grated apples
1 c. nuts	

Combine flour, cinnamon, soda, baking powder and salt. Combine oil, sugar, eggs, vanilla and apples. Stir into flour mixture. Add nuts. Divide into 2 bread pans. Bake at 350° for 40 min. or until done.

Wheat Germ Bread

2 pkg. active dry yeast	1 T. salt
1 c. warm water	½ c. instant potato flakes
(105-130°)	½ tsp. soda
2 c. very warm water	½ c. soft butter or oleo (1 stick)
(120-130°)	1 c. plain wheat germ
½ c. buttermilk powder	6-7½ c. bread flour
¼ c. honey	

Dissolve yeast in warm water. Add rest of ingredients and work in flour. Let rise twice. Bake at 350°. Makes 2-3 loaves.

Orange Pineapple Bread

½ c. firmly packed	2 eggs
brown sugar	½ c. Crisco
4 c. flour, sift	2 tsp. baking soda
¾ tsp. salt	1 - 6 oz. can frozen orange juice, thawed
1 c. chopped nuts	1 - 15¼ oz. Del Monte pineapple
	crushed in its own juice

Cream sugar and shortening until light and fluffy. Add eggs and beat well. Sift together flour, baking soda and salt. Alternately add dry ingredients and orange juice to creamed mixture. Mix well after each addition. Stir in pineapple and nuts. Pour in 2 well-greased and floured pans. Bake at 350° for 50-60 min.

Date Nut Bread

⅔ c. butter	3 eggs
2 c. sugar	½ c. water
1½ c. canned pumpkin	2⅓ c. sifted flour
2 tsp. soda	1 tsp. cinnamon
1 tsp. salt or less	½ tsp. cloves
⅔ c. chopped pecans	⅔ c. cut up dates

Cream butter and sugar. Gradually add eggs, beat well. Blend in water, pumpkin and sifted ingredients. Fold in nuts and dates. Pour into 2 greased loaf pans. Bake at 350° for about 1 hr. Makes 2 loaves.

Virginia Spoon Bread

1 c. white cornmeal	4 T. butter
2 c. boiling water	4 eggs
¾ tsp. salt	1 c. whole milk

Preheat oven to 400°. Pour cornmeal slowly, stirring all the time, into boiling water until mixture is thick and smooth. Add salt and butter; cut in chunks. Stir some more until it is smooth and slick. In another bowl, beat eggs and milk rather vigorously until mixture foams. Beat 2 mixtures together until smooth. Pour into a buttered large casserole. Bake 30-45 min. until knife inserted in middle comes out clean and top is brown.

No-Fail Bread

3 pkg. yeast	1 qt. scalded milk
⅓ c. lukewarm water	1 qt. boiling water
¾ c. sugar	½ c. shortening
2½ T. salt	about 25 c. sifted flour

Soften yeast in lukewarm water. Combine sugar, salt, milk, boiling water and shortening in large bowl; cool to lukewarm. Add yeast and ½ the flour; beat until smooth. Work in enough remaining flour to make easily handled dough. Knead dough until smooth; cover and let rise until doubled in bulk. Punch dough down; shape into 8 loaves (or rolls, if preferred). Place in greased pans; let rise until doubled in bulk. Bake at 400° for 30 min.

Pineapple Bread

¾ c. brown sugar	2 c. flour
3 T. soft butter	2 tsp. baking powder
2 eggs	¼ tsp. baking soda
1 - 8 oz. can crushed	
pineapple	

Pour in a greased loaf pan and sprinkle with cinnamon and sugar. Bake at 350° for one hr. and 10 min.

Cranberry Bread

½ c. raisins
¼ c. coarsely chopped
    walnuts
¼ c. fresh cranberries
    (halved)
1½ c. unsifted flour
    (all-purpose)
½ tsp. baking soda
¼ c. water

½ tsp. ground cinnamon
½ tsp. ground nutmeg
¼ tsp. salt
1 c. cooked, canned or frozen,
    thawed pumpkin or
    yellow winter squash
½ c. cooking or vegetable oil
2 eggs
1 c. firmly packed brown sugar

In bowl, mix together raisins, walnuts and cranberries. Sprinkle with 1 T. of flour and toss to coat evenly. Stir together remaining flour, brown sugar, soda, cinnamon, nutmeg and salt. In large bowl of mixer set at low speed, stir together pumpkin, eggs, oil and water. Gradually stir in flour mixture, scraping sides with rubber scraper as required. Stir in flour coated fruit and nut mixture. Turn batter evenly, into six greased and floured (4½" x 2½" x 1¼") miniature baking pans. Bake in a 350° preheated oven until well browned and cake tester inserted in center of one comes out clean. About 35 min. Turn out on rack and cool. This kitchen tested recipe makes 6 miniature loaves of bread.

Cinnamon Raisin Bread

½ c. sugar
1 c. lard or oil
2 eggs beaten
1 T. cinnamon

2 T. salt
1½ c. hot milk
2 T. yeast in 1 c. warm water

1½-2 c. raisins cooked 5 min. in water to cover; add water if necessary to
    make 5 c. liquid.

10 or 12 c. flour (more if necessary)

Bake at 350° for 40 min. Makes 4 or 5 loaves.

Banana Bread

1 c. sugar
½ c. Crisco or shortening
1 c. very ripe mashed
    bananas
1 egg

1 tsp. soda
¼ tsp. salt
1 c. chopped pecans or walnuts
2 c. flour

Cream shortening and sugar until well blended. Add the beaten egg and beat well. Then add the mashed bananas (3 or 4 bananas make a c.). Mix thoroughly. Add flour, salt, and soda sifted together.

Kentucky Cornbread

½ c. sugar	¾ c. cornmeal
1½ c. flour	2 tsp. baking powder
1 c. milk	¼ c. cooking oil or lard
1 egg	salt

Mix dry ingredients, add the rest, stir and bake at 350°.

Spice Ginger Bread

½ c. veg. oil	½ c. sugar
2½ c. all purpose flour	1 c. baking molasses
1 c. hot water	½ tsp. salt
1 egg	1½ tsp. soda
1½ tsp. ginger	1½ tsp. cinnamon
½ tsp. cloves	

Beat together shortening, sugar, and egg. Sift together flour, soda, salt, and spices. Combine molasses and water; add alternately with dry ingredients to first mixture. Pour in greased 9" x 13" pan and bake in moderate oven.

Apple Bread

1 c. sugar	2 c. Gold Medal flour (self-rising)
½ c. shortening	2 c. chopped, pared apples
2 eggs	½ c. chopped nuts
1 tsp. vanilla	1 T. sugar
¼ tsp. cinnamon	

Heat oven to 350°. Grease and flour a 9" x 5" x 3" loaf pan. Mix 1 c. sugar, shortening, eggs and vanilla. Stir in flour until smooth, stir in apples and nuts. Spread in pan. Mix 1 T. of sugar and cinnamon. Sprinkle over batter. Bake until wooden pick inserted in center comes out clean. 50 to 60 min. Remove from pan immediately. Cool before slicing. Makes 1 loaf.

Rhubarb Bread

½ c. margarine
1 c. white sugar
2 c. flour
1 tsp. soda
1 c. hot cooked rhubarb

2 eggs, beaten
1 tsp. vanilla
½ tsp. salt
2 T. milk

Cream margarine and sugar. Add eggs and milk. Mix in flour, salt and soda. Add vanilla and hot rhubarb. Pour into 9" x 5" x 3" greased loaf pan. Bake 1 hr. at 375° or till done.

Topping:
1 T. margarine, 1 T. flour, 1 tsp. hot water, 1 T. sugar and 1 tsp. cinnamon. Melt margarine in a sm. pan. Add remaining ingredients and stir until well blended. Pour over top.

Pumpkin Nut Bread

2 c. flour
1 tsp. soda
1 tsp. salt
½ tsp. cinnamon
½ c. butter
1 c. sugar

2 eggs
1 c. mashed pumpkin
¼ c. milk
1 tsp. vanilla
1 c. chopped nuts

Mix thoroughly after each addition. Turn into well-greased and floured pans. Bake at 350° 60-70 min. Makes 2 loaves.

Alma's Favorite Rolls

Melt in a large bowl:
2 sticks oleo
⅔ c. sugar (scant)

2 c. milk
4½ tsp. salt

Then add 2 c. of cold water to melted mixture to cool to lukewarm.

Have ready 3 pkg. or 3 round T. of dry yeast in ½ c. lukewarm water. Add to first mixture if cooled. Then add 6 c. flour. Beat and add 6 eggs. Beat again and add 6 more c. of flour. Never add more or less. Use big white cups for measuring and level full. Let rise, stir down, let rise again, then shape and let rise again. Then bake. Makes 8-9 pans of rolls.

Cinnamon Raisin Rolls

1 T. yeast	1 c. lukewarm milk
¼ c. sugar	3 c. flour
1 tsp. salt	2 beaten eggs
¼ c. salad oil or oleo	3 T. melted butter
1 T. cinnamon	½ c. raisins
½ c. brown sugar	1 T. butter
¼ c. water	

Dissolve yeast in milk. Add sugar, 1½ c. flour. When bubbly, add salt, eggs, salad oil and 1½ c. flour. Knead. Let rise until double size. Roll to ¼" thick. Spread with melted butter and sprinkle with cinnamon and raisins. Roll like jelly rolls, cut in ½" slices. Place in greased pans. Let rise till double in size. Just before baking, pour caramel syrup over it (made by bringing to boil the brown sugar, 1 T. butter and water). Bake at 350° for 35 min. Makes 18 rolls.

Dinner Rolls

2 c. scalded milk	½ c. sugar
½ c. warm water	2 c. bread mix
6 c. bread flour	2 tsp. salt
(more or less)	2 pkg. yeast
2 beaten eggs	

Scald milk, add sugar, salt and shortening. Dissolve yeast in warm water. When milk mixture has cooled to lukewarm, add dissolved yeast. Mix thoroughly and add enough flour to make a thin batter and beat until smooth. Cover and set in warm place until light and bubbly. Add beaten eggs and flour to make a stiff dough. Knead until smooth and pliable. Let stand in warm place until double in bulk. Shape into rolls and place in pans. Let rise. Bake at 350° for about 20 min.

Emma's Potato Buns

1 c. sugar	1 T. salt
½ c. shortening	1 c. mashed potatoes
2 c. milk or warm water	1 T. yeast dissolved in water
2 eggs	8 c. flour

Mix as for bread. Shape into rolls and bake in pans.

Sam's Sticky Buns

1½ c. water   1½ c. milk
½ c. shortening   1 heaping tsp. salt
¾ c. sugar   1 pkg. yeast
4 eggs
Flour as much as needed to handle dough (shape into buns).

Sticky Part:
2 c. brown sugar   1 stick margarine
2 c. cream

Measure brown sugar and margarine into a saucepan. Bring to a boil and boil 5 min. Remove from heat and add cream. Pour sauce into pans and put buns on top. Bake at 350°.

Polly's Puffs

2 c. flour   1 tsp. baking powder
2 T. sugar   1 egg
½ tsp. salt

Milk and cream to mix for a thick dough. Drop in hot lard or oil to bake, then dip in frosting.

Frosting:
Cook till soft:
1 c. brown sugar   1 c. cream
1 T. butter

Miracle Biscuits

2 c. self-rising flour   2 T. sugar
2 T. Miracle Whip   ½ tsp. cinnamon
1 c. milk

Stir until well mixed. Drop onto greased cookie sheet. Bake at 375°–12 to 15 min. (until golden brown). Makes 12 biscuits.

Best Ever Cinnamon Rolls

5 c. warm water	4 T. yeast
1½ c. soft lard or oil	7 tsp. salt
4 eggs beaten	2 c. sugar
Approx. 12-13 c. flour	1 tsp. cinnamon in brown sugar
(all purpose)	

Let rise till double, punch down and let rise again. Roll out and spread with melted butter or oleo, sprinkle with cinnamon, then put a generous layer of brown sugar on. Roll up, cut and put in pans, let rise and bake at 350° for approximately 30 min. I use 8" foil pans and put 6 or 7 in a pan. Makes 10-12 pans. Make a thin icing of powdered sugar and milk or water and frost.

Swiss Rolls

2 T. yeast	1½ c. warm water
2 c. scalded milk	¾ c. sugar
1 c. oil or shortening	4 eggs
3 tsp. salt	10 c. flour

Pour hot milk over salt, sugar and shortening in a large bowl. Dissolve yeast in warm water in a smaller bowl. Add eggs to yeast and beat well. When milk mixture is lukewarm, add yeast mixture and beat well. Add 6 c. of flour and beat again. Stir in last 4 c. Let rise until double (1-2 hr.). Divide dough into 4 equal parts. Roll each part into a circle, brush melted butter on dough and cut into 12 pie wedges. Begin rolling up from wide ends and place on baking sheet. Let rise 1 hr. and then bake at 325° for 15 min.

Basic Sweet Rolls

Stir:

1 stick oleo	1 c. sugar
2 pt. hot milk	

Add:

4 eggs (beaten)	2 T. salt

Put 2 T. yeast in 1 c. warm water. Cool milk, then add yeast. Put in order given. Add flour till stiff—about 12 c. Shape as desired.

Raisin Biscuits

¼ c. sugar
2 c. flour
3 T. lard

¼ c. raisins
4 tsp. baking powder
¾-1 c. milk

Sift flour, baking powder and salt together, cup in lard. When the mixture is in lumps the size of peas, add the milk all at once. Mix well together and turn dough out onto a floured board. Rill ¾" thick and cut with biscuit cutter. Bake at 450° for 12 min. Makes 16-18 biscuits. Drop biscuits may be made by adding ¼ c. milk preceding recipe and dropping dough from a spoon onto cookie sheet or into muffin pans. Glaze with frosting.

Cream Drops

About 1 qt. cooking oil
½ c. sugar
½ c. milk
2 tsp. baking powder
powdered sugar (optional)

2 c. flour
½ c. light cream
2 eggs
¼ tsp. soda

Heat oil in saucepan to about 375°. Mix flour, baking powder and soda and sift 3 times. Beat eggs well, add sugar gradually and mix. Add dry ingredients to egg mixture alternately with cream and juice mix. Drop by tablespoons into hot oil and fry about 2½ min. Turn them as soon as they come to the top of the oil, then turn frequently until they are as brown as desired. Drain. Sprinkle with sugar. Makes 2½ doz.

To Glaze Doughnuts

¼ c. cold water
¼ c. boiling water
2 T. melted Crisco

1 pkg. gelatin soaked in ¼ c. cold water
1 box confectioners XXX sugar
1 tsp. vanilla

Put in double boiler and keep over hot water while glazing cooled doughnut; put on long stick and let drip.

So much has been given to me,
I have no time to ponder over that which has been denied.
– Helen Keller

Favorite Doughnuts

Mix together:

1 c. hot water	2 T. sugar
1 stick butter	1 tsp. salt

Then add:

1 c. boiled milk	2 pkg. yeast
3 T. sugar	3 c. flour

Beat well. Add 3 eggs, beat well. Then add 3 more c. flour. This is a very soft doughnut. Let rise only once. Roll on floured board and cut, let rise 20 min. Fry in hot shortening until brown; cool and glaze.

Baking Powder Doughnuts

1 c. sugar	1 c. cream
½ c. milk	3 eggs
3 c. flour	2 tsp. baking powder

Roll out and cut doughnuts and fry in deep fat. I like to roll in sugar.

Mashed Potato Doughnuts

1 c. Crisco	1 c. sugar
1 c. mashed potatoes	2 T. salt
1 qt. milk (scalded)	6 egg yolks
3 T. yeast	13 c. flour

Let rise 1 hr. Roll out, cut; let rise again to almost double. Then deep fry, glaze or frost.

Doughnut Glaze

1 c. butter, melted	2 tsp. vanilla
3 c. powdered sugar	Enough milk for dipping consistency

Keep warm in top of double boiler. Dip doughnuts hot and drain a bit. Wooden spoon handle works nicely.

Molly's Doughnuts

3 eggs well beaten
3 T. melted butter
1 c. milk
4 tsp. baking powder
½ tsp. nutmeg

1 c. sugar
1 tsp. salt
3½ c. sifted flour
1 tsp. vanilla

Beat eggs, add sugar, then milk. Add sifted dry ingredients. Add melted butter. Roll out to ¼" in thickness. Fry in deep fat 2 to 3 min. Drain on brown paper. Roll in sugar and cinnamon.

Cinnamon Doughnuts

2 eggs
1 c. milk
5 tsp. salt
4 tsp. baking powder

1 c. white sugar
4 c. flour
1½ tsp. vanilla
½ tsp. cinnamon

Beat the eggs and sugar together until light, then add milk and vanilla. Sift flour, baking powder and salt together and add to wet mix. Roll this big doughy mess out to ¼" thickness on a floured board. Cut into shape and fry in 380° deep oil on each side for about 3 min. or until nicely browned. Remove from oil and drain on paper towels. Good eating plain, sprinkled with powdered sugar or white sugar and cinnamon.

Minnie's Yeast Doughnuts

Add: 2 pkg. yeast to ½ c. warm water. Let stand.
Scald ¾ c. milk; pour into large bowl with ¼ c. sugar and 1 tsp. salt.
Blend together and cool to lukewarm. Stir yeast mixture well and pour into bowl.

Mix in:
⅓ c. soft shortening   2 eggs
3¼ c. sifted flour

Beat until batter is smooth and cover. Let rise in warm place until doubled, about 30 min. Roll out and cut while fat is heating.

Long Johns

2 pkg. dry yeast soaked in 1 c. warm water

1 c. milk	½ c. butter or oleo
⅔ c. sugar	2 eggs
6 c. flour	1 tsp. salt

Put butter, sugar, eggs and salt into the scalded milk; let cool. Then add to the yeast. Add the flour. Let rise once, roll out and cut. Let rise again. Fry in deep fat or veg. oil. Make a slit in side and fill with filling. Also spread on top.

Filling:
2⅓ c. powdered sugar	¼ tsp. salt
1 egg white beaten	

Mix together and set aside.

Boil 1 minute:
2 T. water	¼ c. white sugar

Add to first mixture. Add:
1 tsp. flavor	½ c. Crisco oil or veg. oil

Grandpa's Doughnuts

2 c. milk	2 c. water
1½ c. shortening	1 T. salt
1 scant c. sugar	3 eggs
5 lb. or less bread flour	3 T. dry yeast (dissolved in water with 1 T. sugar)

Knead 2 or 3 times ½ hr. apart. Roll out and cut with doughnut cutter and fry. Can also be made into rolls and baked.

Luscious Filled Doughnuts

1 qt. milk	1 tsp. sugar
2 c. mashed potatoes	2 eggs, beaten
1 c. shortening	1 tsp. salt
1 c. sugar	9-11 c. flour
3 T. yeast	¾ c. warm water

Cream Filling:

1 c. shortening	2 egg whites
½ c. margarine	1 c. marshmallow creme
1¼ lb. powdered sugar	Enough milk to mix

Scald milk. Add potatoes, shortening and sugar. Cool. Dissolve yeast in water and 1 tsp. sugar. Add to lukewarm milk mixture. Add eggs and salt. Work in flour. Let rise till double. Roll out ½" thick. Cut and let rise till light. Deep-fry till golden brown. Cool. Fill, if desired.

Applesauce Donuts

3 c. white flour	1¼ tsp. cinnamon
1½ c. whole wheat flour	⅔ c. buttermilk
3 tsp. baking powder	½ c. applesauce
1 tsp. soda	¼ c. butter
1 tsp. salt	1 tsp. vanilla
½ tsp. nutmeg	2 eggs, beaten
¼ tsp. cloves	1 c. sugar

Combine first 8 ingredients in large bowl and blend well. Combine remaining ingredients. Mix well. Add to dry ingredients. Stir just till well moistened. Chill dough. On a well-floured surface, toss dough lightly until no longer sticky. Roll dough to ⅜" thickness. Cut with floured doughnut cutter. Deep-fry in hot fat (375°, I use electric skillet) about 1½ min. on each side or till golden brown. Cool slightly. Dust with powdered sugar.

Lightest Ever Doughnuts

2 c. water (lukewarm)	2 eggs, well beaten
1 T. yeast	2 tsp. salt
½ c. vegetable oil	Approximately 6 c. flour
½ c. sugar	

Soften yeast in water. Add next 4 ingredients, then 2 c. flour. Let rise 30 min. Add rest of flour, just enough to work well with your hands. Knead till smooth. Let rise till double. Lay out, do not punch down or use rolling pin, just pat it out and cut. Let rise again. Fry in hot fat, deep enough so doughnuts float. We've had better results with this recipe than any other. This recipe can also be used to make sticky buns.

Hoagie Buns

2 c. lukewarm water	2 eggs
2 T. yeast	½ c. shortening
½ c. sugar	7-7½ c. flour
2 tsp. salt	

Dissolve yeast in 2 c. water. Stir in sugar, salt, eggs and shortening. Gradually stir in flour. Let rise until double. Punch down and shape into buns as desired. Place on cookie sheet. Let rise. Bake at 350° for 20 to 30 min. These are good for "hoagies" or submarine sandwiches.

Today a loaf of bread I'll bake
And with a cheery smile I'll take
It to a home where there is need–
I'm passing on a kindly deed.

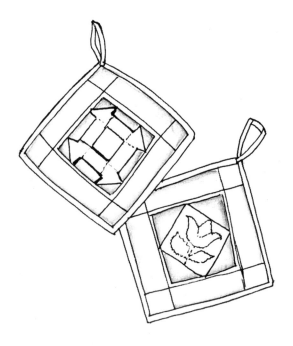

Vegetables and Side Dishes

Going to Grandpa's House

Going to visit Grandpa and Grandma was always a special occasion. It was usually in the evening after the chores were done. Dad would light two lanterns and hang one on each side of the carriage, so we'd have light on the road.

Old Charlie knew the way without being told where to turn. I believe he liked to go there, too, because that was the farm where he had grown up, and several of his "brothers" still lived there. He would whinny joyously to the horses in their stalls and they would whinny a reply.

Grandma always stood at the open door to welcome us, with a big smile on her face and a hug waiting for me and the younger ones. Grandpa liked to tweak our ears and tease us a little. He always mentioned how much we were growing and that we must have hearty appetites. This was Grandma's signal to go to the pantry and bring out platefuls of sugar cookies and molasses tarts which she always kept on hand. She also got down her cut-glass tumblers and served either canned grape juice or cider.

She usually had a quilt in the frame which Mother sat down to help with, and I played with her rag dolls, who were nicely dressed but had no faces. The little boys played with the wooden blocks Grandpa had made, or the marble roller.

All too soon it was time to start for home, and into the carriage we piled again. The rattle of the carriage wheels lulled us to sleep and we had to be roused when we got home. We sleepily stumbled to the house, then climbed the stairs and tumbled into our beds.

Easy Baked Beans

2 - 16 oz. cans baked beans
½ tsp. mustard
2 sm. onions
bacon slices

¼ c. brown sugar
½ c. ketchup
1 tsp. Worcestershire sauce

Stir all together, except bacon. Put in baking dish; top with bacon slices. Bake at 350° for 1 hr.

Baked Beans For a Crowd

3 gal. baked beans
4 big onions
1 lg. bottle ketchup

2 qt. king syrup
salt and pepper
about 2 lb. bacon, fried bacon
       or ham chopped up

Mix all together and bake at 300° for 3 hr.

Stovetop Special

3 c. cooked navy beans

Add:
1 c. cream
½ c. brown sugar
2 tsp. mustard
5 slices velveeta cheese
       (or more)

3 T. butter
½ c. ketchup
1 sm. chopped onion
2 hot dogs, sliced

Cook slowly on top of stove till well heated and cheese is melted; add cut up hot dogs.

Scalloped Corn

2 c. canned or frozen corn
⅔ c. cracker or bread crumbs
½ tsp. salt
1 tsp. sugar
1 tsp. minced onion

1 c. milk
3 T. melted butter
⅛ tsp. pepper
2 eggs

Butter casserole. Bake 350° for 30 min.

Creamed Corn

1 - 16 oz. can creamed corn ¼ c. butter
1 box Jiffy Muffin mix 2 eggs
½ pt. sour cream

Mix altogether. Bake at 350° for 35 min.

Cheesy Potato Bake

10 potatoes 8 oz. Velveeta cheese (diced)
    (cooked, peeled, diced) 1 onion (chopped)
salt and pepper 1 green pepper (chopped)

Mix above ingredients and set aside.

2 slices of bread 1½ c. milk
    (toasted and cubed) ½ c. melted butter

Pour this into a baking dish. Make a topping of 1½ c. cornflakes and ¼ c. butter. Sprinkle topping on top and bake uncovered for 45 min. at 300°.

Mashed Potato Puffs

To about 2 c. leftover mashed potatoes add:
3 eggs ¼ c. sweet milk
2 T. flour ½ tsp. salt

Mix all together and fry as for pancakes till light brown. Eat with a meat gravy or plain.

Cream Cheese Mashed Potatoes

3 lb. potatoes - peeled, ¼ c. onion (chopped fine)
    cooked, mashed 1 - 8 oz. pkg. cream cheese
    and hot (room temperature)
¼ c. butter 2 eggs (beaten)
½ c. sour cream 1 tsp. salt
½ c. milk pepper to taste

Mash potatoes in large bowl. Cut cream cheese in sm. pieces and add to potatoes along with the butter. Beat well until melted. Add sour cream. Mix eggs and milk, then add to potato mixture along with onions, salt and pepper. Beat well. Pour mixture into a greased casserole and refrigerate overnight. Bake at 350° for 45 min.

Velveeta Potatoes

10 lb. cooked and	½ lb. Velveeta cheese
diced potatoes	¾ c. flour
3 tsp. salt	3-4 c. milk
¾ c. butter or oleo	pepper
1 med. onion	

Brown butter and add onions, flour, salt and pepper. Add milk. Heat until thick. Last, add cheese and 3-4 lb. ham (cut). Heat to 350° until steaming, then reduce to 300°. Bake ½ to 1 hr.

Leftover Mashed Potatoes

2 c. mashed potatoes	⅓ c. milk
3 eggs	2-3 slices bread (crumbs)
salt and pepper to taste	1 sm. onion (chopped)

Mix all ingredients together. Pour into a hot buttered skillet. Cover and heat slowly.

Scalloped Cabbage

1 lb. cabbage, coarsely	5 T. margarine
shredded	1 c. milk
2 qt. boiling water	3 T. flour
¼ c. salt	1 c. buttered soda cracker crumbs

Cook cabbage in boiling water seasoned with salt for 4 min. Be careful not to overcook. Drain well. Place in buttered 2 qt. flat casserole. Make a cream sauce with butter, flour and milk and pour over cabbage. Sprinkle with buttered cracker crumbs on top. Bake at 325° for 45 min. This same recipe may be used with broccoli instead of cabbage.

Baked Sauerkraut

1 lg. can sauerkraut, rinsed
1 can tomatoes, snipped
    into sm. pieces

1 c. brown sugar
4-6 slices fried bacon (crumbled)

Combine all ingredients in a slightly greased casserole. Sprinkle with bread crumbs and grated cheese. Bake 1 hr. at 350°.

Sauerkraut Rolls

4 T. melted margarine
1 onion (chopped fine
    and browned)

4 T. flour
1½ c. ham, chopped fine

Cook the above ingredients in large skillet a few min. Add: ½ c. ham broth, 3 c. sauerkraut, drained and chopped and 1 T. parsley (optional). Let cool. Shape into 1" balls. Beat 1 egg; then add ½ c. milk. Dip balls into 1 c. flour; then into egg and milk mixture; then roll in bread crumbs. Fry in deep fat at 375° until nicely browned. Drain and serve.

Broccoli Mushroom Bake

1 - 10 oz. pkg. of frozen
    broccoli, cut
    or chopped
1 tsp. margarine

½ - 10½ oz. can cream of mushroom soup
1 oz. grated cheddar cheese
2 T. dry bread crumbs

1) Preheat oven to 350°.
2) Cook broccoli until tender crisp, drain.
3) Stir in soup and cheese. Pour into a 1 qt. baking dish.
4) Melt margarine in sm. skillet over med. heat, add bread crumbs.
    Stir until lightly browned. Sprinkle bread crumbs over casserole.
5) Bake 25 to 30 min. Serving size ½ c.

Breaded Cauliflower

Clean cauliflower by removing leaves and the core. Place on a steam rack with a cup of water or enough to cover bottom of pan. Squeeze ½ lemon juice and all into the pan. Cover and steam only until a fork pierces the cauliflower easily. Do not overcook. Meanwhile, melt ½ stick of butter in a saucepan and brown 1 c. of bread crumbs lightly. Remove cauliflower and break into flowerettes. Place in pan with buttered bread crumbs and continue to turn until the cauliflower is well coated. Serve hot.

Salsify Bake

2 c. of cooked salsify	3 c. crushed crackers
(oyster plant)	2 eggs
2 T. butter	⅛ tsp. pepper
1 tsp. salt	3 c. milk

Wash salsify and cook until soft. Peel and cut in sm. pieces. Put in layers of cracker crumbs and salsify. Sprinkle with salt and pepper. Have cracker crumbs on top. Beat eggs, add milk and pour over ingredients. Dot with butter. Bake at 350° about 45 min. Serves 6.

Bisquick Zucchini

3 c. peeled chopped	1 c. Bisquick
zucchini	½ c. cheese (velveeta)
½ c. oil	½ tsp. garlic powder
1 tsp. salt	chopped onion
4 eggs	

Mix together in casserole. Bake at 350° for 30-40 min.

Creamed Cauliflower

¼ tsp. pepper	1 lg. head cauliflower
½ tsp. salt	3 hard cooked eggs
1 c. buttered bread crumbs	¼ c. grated cheese
2 c. med. white sauce	

Break the head of cauliflower into flowerettes and cook in salt water until tender. Place alternate layers of cauliflower, diced egg and white sauce in a greased casserole. Put a layer of buttered bread crumbs and grated cheese on top. Bake at 375° for 25 min. You may want to melt the cheese in the white sauce and use only crumbs on top.

Zucchini Patties

2 med. zucchini (grated)   2 T. minced onion
½ c. flour   1 tsp. salt
2 T. minced parsley   1 grated carrot
1 egg (beaten)   dash of pepper

In colander, mix zucchini and salt, let drain about 15 min., squeezing out excess liquid with back of spoon. Mix well: drained zucchini (about 1 c.), onion, parsley, carrot, egg, flour and pepper. Drop by tablespoons into ½" hot oil in skillet and fry until brown on both sides. Drain on absorbent paper and serve hot.

Sweet 'N Sour Dandelion

1 c. crumbled fried bacon   1 qt. dandelion greens

Fry and add 1 c. milk. Make thick sauce with 3 T. flour, 2 T. brown sugar, a little vinegar. Put washed, cut up dandelion greens in a bowl. When ready to eat, pour the hot sauce over it. Do not cook dandelions. Add 2 hard boiled eggs, cut up. Spinach may also be used.

Cabbage Cheese Bake

1 med. head of cabbage,   ¼ c. butter
    cut into 8 wedges   ⅛ tsp. pepper
¼ c. finely chopped   ½ c. mayonnaise
    green peppers   ½ c. shredded cheddar cheese
2 c. milk   ¼ c. flour
¼ c. finely chopped onion

In a covered Dutch oven or large skillet, cook cabbage in small amount of water about 12 min. Drain. Place in 13" x 9" baking dish. In saucepan cook peppers and onion in butter until tender. Blend in flour, salt and pepper. Add milk; cook and stir till bubbly. Pour over cabbage. Bake uncovered in 375° oven for 20 min. Combine cheese and mayonnaise and spoon on wedges. Bake 5 more min.

Broccoli Casserole

Cook fresh or frozen cut broccoli, and drain. Stir in velveeta cheese whiz or cheddar cheese and a little milk. Put in a casserole and put crushed ritz crackers on top. Bake.

Broccoli Rice Supreme

½ c. chopped onions	2 pkg. (10 oz. each)
3 c. hot cooked rice	frozen chopped broccoli
6 eggs	1½ c. grated sharp cheddar cheese (6 oz.)
1 tsp. salt	½ c. milk
¼ tsp. pepper	1 can sliced mushrooms (drained)

Cook onions with broccoli according to directions on package of broccoli. Drain well and set aside. Combine: rice, ¾ c. cheese, 2 eggs slightly beaten, and ½ tsp. salt. Press firmly and evenly over bottom and sides of a greased 12" pizza pan or two 9" pie pans. Beat remaining eggs slightly. Stir in milk, pepper, mushrooms and remaining salt. Add to broccoli and mix well. Spoon onto crust. Bake in 375° oven for 20 min. Sprinkle with remaining cheese. Bake 10 min. longer. Cool a few min. before serving.

Broccoli Wonder

1 lb. fresh broccoli	1 T. vinegar
1 T. salad oil	1 T. sesame seed, toasted
1 T. soy sauce	4 tsp. sugar

Cook broccoli in small amount of boiling salted water about 15 min., or just until tender; drain. In a sm. saucepan, combine oil, vinegar, soy sauce, sugar, and sesame seed; heat to boiling. Pour sauce over hot broccoli turning spears to coat. Serve immediately. Makes 4 to 5 servings.

Mixed Vegetable Bake

1 - 16 oz. jar lima beans, drained	½ tsp. celery salt
	5 T. butter
1 - 16 oz. jar whole kernel corn, drained	½ tsp. onion salt
	1 - 16 oz. jar whole tomatoes, drained

In a 1½ qt. casserole combine all ingredients except butter. Dot surface with butter. Bake in moderate oven for ½ hr. or until done.

Acorn Squash Bake

1 med. acorn squash
2 sm. apples, peeled
   and diced
2 tsp. minced onion

2 tsp. margarine (melted)
2 T. water
dash of salt
2 T. diced celery

(1) Preheat oven to 400° F.
(2) Cut squash in half, remove seeds and place cut side down on cookie sheet sprayed with pan spray.
(3) Combine apples, celery and onion. Add margarine and water. Put in sm. baking dish. Cover.
(4) Bake squash and apple stuffing for 45 min. or till tender. Remove from oven.
(5) Salt squash and fill with apple mixture.

Veggie Tater Dish

2 bags tater tots
4 c. mixed vegetables
1 can cream of chicken soup

1 lb. hamburger
1 can cream of mushroom soup

Brown hamburger, then mix soups, vegetables and meat together. Put a bag of tater tots in bottom of pan or roaster; spread mixture over tater tots, then put other bag on top. Put cheese on top. Bake till very bubbly.

Beany Mushroom Bake

1½ lb. hamburger
1 qt. green beans
1 can cream of
   mushroom soup

1 med. onion
salt and pepper to taste
Processed American or Velveeta cheese

Fry hamburger and onion until hamburger is brown and onion tender. Add salt, pepper and soup. Mix and heat until hot. Layer green beans, hamburger mixture and put cheese on top. Bake at 350° for 1 hr. This casserole can also be frozen.

Sour Cream Lima Bake

4 cans (or 6 c.) limas
1 T. prepared mustard
1 c. sour cream

1 c. brown sugar
1 T. dark molasses
½ tsp. salt - dash of pepper

Rinse and drain lima beans. Mix all other ingredients. Stir all together and pour in baking dish. Bake 1 hr. at 350°.

Carrot Tomato Bake

2 lb. carrots. diced
  and cooked
1 green pepper, sliced
¾ c. vinegar
1 tsp. dry mustard

1 onion, sliced in rings
¾ c. sugar
1 tsp. Worcestershire sauce
½ c. vegetable oil
1 can tomato soup

Mix all together. Marinate in refrigerator overnight. Serve cold.

Carrot Fritters

3 c. grated carrots
3 eggs
cracker crumbs

1 sm. onion
pinch of salt and pepper

Drop in hot butter or lard by tablespoons and fry on both sides.

Onion Fritters

¾ c. flour
1 T. sugar
1 T. cornmeal

2 tsp. baking powder
1 tsp. salt
2½ c. fine chopped onions

Mix first 5 ingredients. Stir in enough milk (or water if ½ c. powdered milk is used) to make a thick batter. Mix in onions, chopped fine, and drop by spoonfuls into deep fat. Flatten patties slightly as you turn them. Fry to a golden brown. Deep fat should be heated to 350° before adding batter.

Onion Pepper Carrots

2. lb. carrots
1 med. onion
½ c. oil
¾ c. vinegar
1 tsp. Worcestershire sauce

1 sm. green pepper, thinly sliced
1 - 10 oz. can condensed tomato soup
1 c. sugar
1 tsp. prepared mustard
salt and pepper to taste

Cook carrots 5 min., then drain. Combine with other vegetables, set aside. Combine all other ingredients, bring to a boil and pour over vegetables; mix well. Marinate at least 10-12 hr.

Curried Eggplant

1 med. eggplant (1½ lb.)
1 c. all-purpose flour
1 tsp. tumeric
1 c. milk
1 egg

1 tsp. salt
1 tsp. baking powder
1 tsp. curry powder
¼ c. salad oil

Wash eggplant. Beat remaining ingredients with rotary beater until smooth. Heat fat or oil (1" deep) to 375° in large skillet. Peel and cut eggplant into ¼" slices. Dip slices into batter, letting excess drip into bowl. Fry in hot fat until golden brown, turning once. Drain. If desired, salt to taste. Makes 4 servings. Note: To keep fried eggplant slices warm and crisp, place in 400° oven until ready to serve.

Good Cream of Mushroom Patties

1 can cream of
   mushroom soup
2 tsp. beef broth flavor

2 c. quick oatmeal
3 eggs
1 sm. onion or powder sage

Mix together and fry in buttered frying pan.

Sweet Potato Surprise

1 can (1 lb. 13 oz.) sweet
   potato pieces in syrup
½ c. honey
2 T. butter

½ tsp. vanilla
½ tsp. salt
¾ c. prepared mince meat
½ c. coarsely chopped nuts or
   fine rolled, if desired

Drain sweet potatoes, reserving liquid. Cook syrup down to about ½ c. Add butter, vanilla and honey. Simmer 5 min. Add mince meat, salt and sweet potatoes. Simmer 15 min., basting occasionally with sauce.

Spinach and Bacon

2 lb. spinach	2 eggs (beaten)
2 c. milk	2 c. bread (cubed)
4 T. butter (melted)	¾ tsp. salt
⅛ tsp. pepper	½ c. bacon (cooked)

Cook and drain spinach. Add rest of ingredients except bacon. Place in greased casserole and put bacon on top. Bake at 350° for 40 min. Serves 6.

Velveeta Baked Macaroni

4 c. uncooked macaroni	2 tsp. Worcestershire sauce
2 c. Velveeta cheese	6 c. milk
1 tsp. salt	paprika

Put in oven. Bake at 350° for 50 min.

Noodle Crumb Bake

6 oz. noodles	1 c. chicken
1 c. bread crumbs,	1 can mushroom soup
browned in butter	1 c. milk

Cook noodles in salt water until tender. Combine cooked noodles with chicken and mushroom soup and milk. Put in casserole, cover with bread crumbs and bake for 25 min.

Bisquick Zucchini

4 c. shredded zucchini	1 c. Bisquick
½ c. oil	½ c. chopped onions
3 eggs	2 tsp. parsley
1 tsp. oregano	

Bake at 350° for 20-25 min. Then cover with pizza sauce and sprinkle cheese on top. Bake 10 more min.

Spaghetti Supreme

2 slices bacon (diced)
1 tsp. salt
2 med. onions (chopped)
½ lb. spaghetti
1 clove garlic (minced)
1 c. grated cheddar cheese

1 tsp. chili powder
2½ c. water
½ lb. ground beef
2 - 8 oz. cans tomato sauce
pepper to taste

In heavy skillet, fry bacon brown and remove bacon. Add onions and garlic; cook until soft; add meat. Cook and stir until meat loses red color; stir in seasoning salt, pepper and chili powder, and tomato sauce and water. Cover and simmer for 25 min. Put cooked spaghetti and sauce and cheese in layers; cover with lid or foil; bake 30 min.; uncover and bake for 15 min. more in 350° oven.

Cheese Whiz Macaroni

In a 1½ qt. casserole, mix:
½ c. milk
2 c. diced cooked ham
½ c. cheese whiz

1 can cream of chicken soup
2 c. drained cooked macaroni

Bake at 375° for 25 min.

Stovetop Noodles Deluxe

1 lb. browned ground beef
½ green pepper,
    chopped (optional)
2 cloves of garlic
1 tsp. chili powder
large can tomatoes

1 onion, chopped
1 tsp. salt
1 can black olives and liquid (sliced)
1 can corn liquid
8 oz. noodles

Cover and cook ½ hr. on top of stove. Add ½ lb. shredded cheddar cheese. Cover and cook till cheese melts.

Creamette Spaghetti Supreme

1 - 7 oz. package creamette
    spaghetti, uncooked
½ c. skim milk
1 med. onion, chopped

1 egg beaten
vegetable cooking spray
½ lb. lean ground beef
1 med. green pepper, chopped

1 clove garlic, minced
2 c. shredded part skim
    mozzarella cheese
pepperoni
1 tsp. Italian seasoning

1 - 15 oz. can tomato sauce
1 tsp. any salt free herb seasoning
¼ tsp. pepper
2 c. fresh sliced mushrooms

Prepare creamette spaghetti as package directs; drain. In med. bowl, blend milk and egg; add spaghetti and toss to coat. Spray 15" x 10" jelly roll pan with vegetable cooking spray. Spread spaghetti mixture evenly in prepared pan; top with pepperoni. In large skillet cook beef, onion, green pepper and garlic until beef is no longer pink; drain. Add tomato sauce and seasonings; simmer 5 min. Spoon meat mixture evenly over spaghetti. Top with mushrooms and cheese. Bake in 350° oven for 20 min. Let stand 5 min. before cutting. Refrigerate leftovers. Makes 8 servings.

Filling Casserole

1 avg. size chicken,
    cut up (fryer)
1 c. diced carrots (cooked)
1 loaf bread, cubed

1 med. onion (chopped)
2 c. milk
salt and pepper to taste
1 egg

Beat together egg and milk. Roll raw chicken pieces in flour and fry lightly in butter. Arrange chicken in bottom of roasting pan. Bake uncovered for 1 hr. at 450°. (For older chickens, add some water and bake longer.) Mix the vegetables, bread cubes, and milk and egg together. Spread on top of chicken. Top with dots of butter. Bake ½ hr. longer.

Four things to keep:
Keep the commandments of the Lord.
Keep thyself in the love of God.
Keep thy lips from speaking guile;
Keep thy feet from the way of evil.

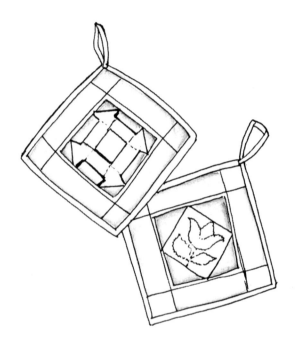

Meats and Casseroles

School Lunches

The one-room school we attended was a mile up the road, so we chose to pack our lunches instead of coming home to eat. We thought we'd rather have more time to play, at noon recess than make the 2 mile round trip. Every fall when school started, packing lunches was fun for awhile, especially if we had a new lunchbox or Thermos bottle. We put in thick sandwiches made of homemade bread, dried beef or bologna, *shmear case* (cup cheese) and fall lettuce. Also big red apples from the orchard, bunches of purple grapes from the vine, or dried apple slices taken while still warm off the drying pan. In the wintertime, we put hearty homemade soups into the Thermos bottle.

I always made sure I had time to stir up a batch of cookies or bars in the evening, for they were so much handier to put in lunch boxes than crumbly cake or juicy fruit pie.

I remember how disappointed I once was when, at noontime I went to the shelf for my lunch and discovered that I had forgotten to bring it to school! The horses had gotten out that morning (my brother left the gate open) and we had a merry chase getting them back in. It almost made us late for school, which was why I forgot my lunch. I was overjoyed when, through the window I saw my brother coming a-galloping on horseback to bring my lunch to school. (I forgave him then for forgetting to close the gate.)

The food tasted extra good that time, and I had to think of what an old-timer in our neighborhood used to say. He said that when he was a boy, they were so dirt-poor that all he had in his lunch at school were slices of cold mush leftover from breakfast, and coarse apple butter bread (*lattvarrick brote*). He would duck down behind the lid of his lunchbox to eat so no one would see what he had to eat. He was always the first to run out to play, for seeing the others munch on their goodies increased his hunger pangs. It must not have done him very much harm to go hungry, for he grew up, married, and had 15 children and over 100 grandchildren.

Chicken and Dumplings

4 lb. stewing chicken,   4 c. water
    cut up
1 T. salt

Thicken with:
¾ c. flour   1 c. water
2 tsp. savory

Cook chicken till tender. Remove pieces and thicken with flour and water. Bring to a boil and simmer while preparing batter for dumplings.

1 c. sifted flour   1½ tsp. baking powder
½ tsp. salt   2 T. butter
4 tsp. parsley flakes   1 beaten egg
¼-½ c. milk

Mix dry ingredients. Chop in butter and blend to make crumbs. Blend in milk and beaten egg mixed stirring as little as possible to mix for light dumplings. Drop into chicken mixture by tablespoon. and simmer covered 15 min., then uncovered 5 min. Serve as soon as possible. Diced potatoes, carrots, celery and onions may be added to chicken broth.

Finger Licken' Chicken

2 c. stale bread crumbs   1 c. melted butter or margarine
    grated or substitute   2 tsp. salt
    cracker crumbs   1 clove garlic, crushed
¾ c. grated parmesan cheese   1 or 2 fryers, cut up
¼ c. chopped parsley   ⅛ tsp. pepper

Mix bread or cracker crumbs, cheese, garlic, parsley, salt and pepper. Dip chicken pieces in butter, then in crumb mixture, coating well. Arrange in open shallow pan. Pour remaining butter over all. Bake at 350° for 1 hr. or until tender when pricked with a fork. Baste frequently with drippings.

*It's a happy home where the only scraps are those
left over on the dinner table for the dog.*

Mustard Chicken

½ c. flour
1 tsp. pepper
3 tsp. salt

2 tsp. paprika
¼ tsp. dry mustard

Mix together ingredients, roll cut up raw chicken in mixture. Bake at 350° for 1½ hr.

Skillet Chicken

1 - 3 lb. ready to cook
    broiler-fryer, cut up
1 tsp. salt
1 egg, slightly beaten
3 T. parmesan cheese

¾ c. milk
1 pkg. frozen broccoli spears
⅓ c. butter or margarine
¼ tsp. pepper
1¼ c. fine (cheese) cracker crumbs

Dip pieces of chicken into combined egg and milk mixture, then into cracker crumb mixture. Melt butter then brown chicken in butter over med. flame and cover. When steam escapes, turn to simmer and cook 25 to 30 min. Arrange broccoli over chicken; season, sprinkle with parmesan cheese. Cover tightly, bring to steaming again. Turn to simmer again and cook about 20 min. until broccoli is tender. Makes 4 to 6 servings.

Parmesan Chicken

Young frying chicken, cut up

Mix together:
2 c. crushed cornflakes
1 tsp. paprika
1 tsp. salt

¼ c. parmesan cheese
1 tsp. dry mustard
½ tsp. dry pepper

Melt 2 T. butter in baking dish; dust chicken with flour, dip in a mixture of 2 beaten eggs and ½ c. cream. Roll in crumb mixture, coat well. Lay skin side down in baking dish. Bake at 375° for 1½ hr. or until done.

Accent Chicken

½ c. flour
1 tsp. pepper
3 tsp. salt

1 tsp. accent
1 cut up broiler or young chicken

Mix dry ingredients well in plastic bag and then dust cut up chicken parts. In cake pan melt ¼ lb. butter. Place in pan chicken parts, not crowding. Bake at 350° for 1½-2 hr. or until done.

Chicken Deluxe

Mix together:

1 egg	½ c. water

Mix the following ingredients:

1 c. flour	2 tsp. salt
1 tsp. baking powder	2 tsp. paprika
a little pepper	

Dip chicken into egg mixture, then into flour. Place chicken on cookie sheet in which ¼ lb. butter has been melted. Do not place chicken pieces on top of each other. Bake for 1½ hr. in 350° oven. Bake on one side 45 min. and then turn and bake on other side 45 min. longer.

Amanda's Baked Chicken

1 broiler, cut in pieces	1 c. cornflake crumbs
1½ tsp. salt	⅛ tsp. pepper
½ c. milk	

Combine cornflake crumbs with salt and pepper. Dip chicken in milk, then in crumbs; put foil on cookie sheet, then chicken (only one layer). Bake 1½ hr. Don't turn meat while roasting; leave uncovered.

Chicken and Rice

1 c. natural brown rice (uncooked)	1 can cream of chicken soup
	1 can cream of mushroom soup
1 chicken cut up or 6-8 of your favorite pieces (uncooked)	2 soup cans of water
	⅛ tsp. pepper
	1 sm. onion (chopped)
1 - 4 oz. can mushrooms stems and pieces	paprika

Spread rice in a well-greased roaster. Mix soup, water, onion, pepper and mushroom pieces together and pour over rice. Place chicken pieces over rice and sprinkle with paprika. Bake in a 350° oven for 2½ hr. covered.

Chicken Supreme

The cooked meat of
  1 chicken
1 c. cheese
1 tsp. oregano
½ c. sm. curd cottage
  cheese
¼ tsp. pepper

2 tsp. salt
1 c. milk
1 - 6 oz. can tomato paste
½ tsp. basil leaves
⅔ c. bisquick
2 eggs

Combine all ingredients and bake at 350° for approx. 30 min.

Chicken and Veggies

1 lb. chicken or
  turkey breast
¼ head cabbage

med. head broccoli
2 stalks celery
2 sm. carrots

Other vegetables optional (onion, mushrooms, canned water chestnuts, sugar snap peas, chinese cabbage)

Slice chicken into thin strips. Chop vegetables coarsely. Heat 2 T. oil in nonstick skillet. Slightly brown chicken strips before adding vegetables. Stir fry vegetables until tender-crisp.

Sauce:
1 c. chicken broth   3 T. soy sauce

Thicken with 2 T. cornstarch. Pour over stir-fried vegetables. Serve with hot rice, additional soy sauce and chow mein noodles.

No Peek Chicken

6 chicken breasts
  (remove skin
  and debone)
1 c. herb rice (uncooked)

1 can mushroom soup
1 can celery soup
1 c. milk
1 pkg. onion soup mix (dry)

Mix all ingredients except onion soup. Sprinkle dry onion soup on top. Cover with foil. Bake 1½ hr. at 350°.

Barbecued Chicken

(For a large group of people)

4 c. catsup	1 c. lemon juice
¼ c. minced onion	1 c. melted margarine
1 c. Worcestershire sauce	1 tsp. pepper
8 chickens cut up	

Put the catsup, lemon juice, onion, margarine, sauce and pepper in a huge kettle and bring almost to a boil. Add chicken and stir the pieces around in the sauce. Cover and simmer 25 min., stirring occasionally. Then take the kettle outside to the hot coals and finish the chicken by putting the half-cooked pieces on the grill. Do not paint with anymore sauce.

Picnic Chicken

1 loaf bread (standard size), toast and break up
3 chicken breasts and 3 legs and thighs (pan boil long enough to take off
      bone, in 1 pt. water)

1 can cream of celery soup	4 eggs (beaten lightly)
1 can cream of chicken soup	add soup with 2 c. water
1 scant T. dried parsley	season to taste

Add all together and mix with bread and chicken. Bake approx. 1 hr. at 325°.

Velvet Chicken Casserole

18 slices of bread, toasted and cut in quarters	3 or 4 c. cooked chicken or turkey, cut in pieces
1 can mushrooms, fried in butter	Velveeta cheese
	2 cans cream of celery soup

Fix this in layers. Mix together: 4 eggs, well beaten, 2 c. chicken or turkey broth or gravy, ½ c. milk, ½ c. salad dressing. Pour this on bread. Bake in oven at 350° for 1¼ hr.

Baked Chicken Barbecue

2 - 2 lb. chickens
1 onion (chopped)
oil or fat for browning
2 T. brown sugar
2 T. vinegar
¼ c. lemon juice
1 c. catsup
1 c. water

dash of Tabasco sauce
dash of red pepper
½ T. prepared mustard
3 T. Worcestershire sauce
½ c. chopped celery
1 T. bottled smoke
2 cloves of garlic powder

Cut chicken and brown in fat. Place in a large baking dish. Brown chopped onion and celery in same fat. Add remaining ingredients to onion and celery and let simmer 15 min. Pour over chicken and bake 1½ hr. uncovered in 325° oven. There will be plenty of gravy with the chicken to serve on rice. This dish takes a little extra effort, but is well worth it. (For those of you who do not care to have it so spicy, use less sauce, mustard and smoke.)

Impossible Turkey Pie

2 c. cut up cooked turkey
½ tsp. salt
1 c. shredded natural
    Swiss cheese
3 eggs

1 jar sliced mushrooms, drained
½ c. sliced green onions
1½ c. milk
¾ c. Bisquick

Heat oven to 400°. Grease a casserole with a little butter or oleo. Sprinkle turkey, mushrooms, onions, salt and cheese in dish. Beat remaining ingredients until smooth, about one minute, with a hand mixer. Pour over the other ingredients in casserole. Bake until knife inserted between center and edge comes out clean. About 30 to 35 min. Cool 5 min. Serves 6 to 8.

Fried Chicken

Fry chicken as usual, then dip in a mixture of:

½ c. vinegar
½ c. melted oleo

½ c. water
1 tsp. Worcestershire sauce

Put on tray or cookie sheets and bake ½ hr. or until done.

Lizzie's Chicken Croquettes

2 T. margarine   2½ T. flour
1 c. milk

Make a white sauce and add:

crushed cracker crumbs   2 c. chopped chicken or turkey
a little pepper   2 eggs, beaten
1 tsp. salt

Cool thoroughly. Shape into croquettes, dip in cracker crumbs, then into eggs, then in cracker crumbs again. Fry in vegetable oil.

Favorite Chicken Croquettes

2 T. butter   2½ T. flour
1 c. milk   3 c. minced cooked chicken
1 tsp. salt   ¼ tsp. onion juice
⅛ tsp. pepper   2 T. minced parsley or celery
4 eggs (beaten)   2 c. diced bread crumbs

Melt butter in saucepan, add flour and seasoning; then slowly add milk till a paste is formed. Add chicken and seasoning. Cool thoroughly, roll in crumbs, then beaten eggs and crumbs again. Deep fry.

Delicious Chicken Casserole

Fill bottom of casserole with broken bread

4 c. cooled chicken   1 c. cream of mushroom
¼ c. melted butter   ½ c. salad dressing
4 eggs, well beaten   2 c. milk
1 tsp. salt and pepper   enough cheese to cover
    and celery salt   2 cans celery soup

Bake 350° for 1¼ hr.

Shake and Bake

¾ c. cornflake crumbs
1 tsp. paprika
¼ tsp. black pepper

2 tsp. salt
¼ tsp. dry mustard
1 - 4 or 5 lb. fryer

Coat meat with crumbs and put in roast pan. You can put 2 layers in. Add a little water, cover and bake at 375° for 2½ hr. or until done.

Ground Turkey Deluxe

1¼ lb. ground turkey
1 c. eggplant, diced
1 onion, chopped
6-8 mushrooms, chopped
1 whole egg, beaten
⅓ tsp. sage
⅓ tsp. tarragon
2 T. low sodium tomato sauce

2 c. bran flakes cereal
1 med. bell pepper, chopped
2 med. tomatoes, peeled and chopped
1 egg white, beaten
⅓ tsp. oregano
1 clove garlic
¼ tsp. pepper

Place all of the ingredients, except the tomato sauce, in a large mixing bowl. Mix well until all ingredients are well incorporated. Press mixture in a Pyrex loaf pan 8" x 5" x 3". Spread the tomato sauce evenly over top of loaf. Bake at 350° for 30 min. Remove from oven and drain off excess liquid. Return to oven for additional 45 min. or until loaf is done. Allow to set a few min. before removing from pan and slicing.

Tasty Meatloaf

1 can golden mushroom soup
½ c. fine dry bread crumbs
1 egg slightly beaten
⅓ c. water

2 lb. ground beef
⅓ c. finely chopped onions
1 tsp. salt

Mix thoroughly: ½ c. soup, bread crumbs, beef, onion, egg and salt. Shape into loaf (8" x 4"). Place in shallow baking pan. Bake at 375° for 1 hr. and 15 min. Blend remaining soup, water and 2-3 T. drippings; heat; stir occasionally. Serve with loaf.

Cheddar Cheese Meatloaf

2 c. rice (cooked)
2 cans mushroom soup
1 sm. onion
2 c. taco sauce, mild

2 lb. ground beef
2 c. cheddar cheese (grated)
1 sm. green pepper
corn chips

Brown meat with salt, pepper, onion, and green pepper. Drain. Stir in soup. In a greased 9" x 13" pan begin layering ingredients starting with corn chips (enough to cover bottom) then meat, rice, taco sauce and cheese. Continue layering until all ingredients are used. Cover with foil and bake at 350° for 45 min.

Mamie's Meatloaf

1½ lb. hamburger
½ c. fresh bread crumbs
2 eggs beaten
½ c. chopped onions
1 T. lemon juice

1 tsp. salt
¼ tsp. pepper
18 oz. can tomato sauce with tomato bits
3 T. brown sugar
½ c. catsup

Gently combine beef mix, bread crumbs, eggs, onion, salt and pepper with ⅓ c. tomato sauce. Shape into loaf and bake in shallow pan in 350° oven for 1hr. Pour off any accumulated fat.

For topping: combine remaining tomato sauce, catsup, brown sugar and lemon juice. Pour over loaf and bake 10 min. longer.

Pizza Sauce Meatloaf

1½ lb. hamburger
¾ c. quick rolled oats
¼ c. onion (chopped)
1 egg (beaten)

1½ tsp. salt
¼ tsp. pepper
¾ c. milk
½ c. pizza sauce

Mix ingredients well and pack firmly in a baking dish. Mix the following sauce and pour over meatloaf: ⅓ c. catsup, 2 T. brown sugar and 1 T. mustard. Bake at 350° for 1¼ hr.

Dried Beef Bake

2 cans cream of
    mushroom soup
2 c. Velveeta cheese
2 sliced hard boiled eggs

2¾ c. milk
1¾ c. uncooked macaroni
½ lb. dried beef (chopped)

Directions: Stir soup until creamy. Add milk, cheese, macaroni and diced beef. Fold in egg slices. Pour into buttered dish. Refrigerate 3-4 hr. Bake 1 hr. uncovered in 350° oven.

Montana Meatballs

1 lb. ground beef
⅓ c. milk
¼ c. chopped onion
1¼ tsp. salt
1 can cream of chicken soup

¼ c. uncooked rice
⅛ tsp. pepper
¼ c. cracker crumbs
2 T. shortening

Combine all ingredients except shortening and soup. Shape in sm. balls, brown in shortening. Dilute soup with 1 can water, pour over meatballs. Cover and simmer for 1 hr. and 15 min.

Saucy Meatballs

1 c. bread crumbs
½ c. milk
⅛ tsp. pepper

1 lb. ground beef
1 tsp. salt

Sauce:
¾ c. ketchup
sm. onion (chopped)
¼ c. vinegar

1 tsp. Worcestershire sauce
¾ tsp. salt
1 c. water

Mix meat and shape into balls; put in baking dish and pour over the sauce and bake. Bake at 350° for 1 hr.

Adam and Eve had an ideal marriage;
he didn't have to hear about all the men she could have married;
she didn't have to hear about the way his mother cooked it.

Taco Burgers

1 lb. ground beef
8 hamburger buns split and toasted
1 - 10 oz. can Old El Paso tomatoes and green chilies
1 envelope Taco seasoning mix
2 c. shredded lettuce
¼ c. water
1 c. (4 oz.) shredded American or Monterey Jack cheese
1 tomato, peeled and chopped

Brown meat; drain fat. Stir in El Paso tomatoes and green chilies, taco seasoning mix and water. Simmer uncovered till thick, about 15 min. Stir in chopped tomatoes. Heat; spoon on buns. Top with lettuce and cheese.

Tomato Burgers

Crumble 2 lb. hamburger in a frying pan. (10½")
Cut fine 2 onions and add to meat. Let fry till juice disappears.
Add enough tomato juice to almost cover meat. Let cook a while.

Add:
1 tsp. mustard   salt and pepper
Add enough rolled oats or flour to thicken for sandwiches.

Bisquick Beef Bake

1 lb. ground beef	3 eggs
1½ c. chopped onions	2 tomatoes (sliced)
½ tsp. salt	1 c. shredded cheddar
¼ tsp. pepper	or process American
1½ c. milk	cheese (I use Velveeta cheese)
¾ c. Bisquick (baking mix)	

Heat oven to 400°. Grease pie plate 10" x 1½". Brown beef and onions; drain. Stir in salt and pepper. Spread in plate. Beat milk, baking mix and eggs until smooth. Pour into plate on meat. Bake 25 min. Top with tomatoes and cheese. Bake until knife inserted comes out clean, 5 to 8 min. Serves 6 to 8.

PA Dutch Meatballs

1½ lb. ground beef
½ c. milk
1 tsp. salt
½ tsp. pepper

1 c. oatmeal
1 med. onion, chopped fine
1 can cream of mushroom soup
    mixed with 1 c. milk

Mix ground beef with all ingredients except soup and milk. Form into sm. balls. Brown meatballs in margarine. Place in casserole and add the soup and milk mixture. Bake in 325° oven for 1 hr.

Swedish Meatballs

1 lb. ground beef
⅓ c. bread crumbs
1 egg
½ T. salt

⅓ c. milk
2 T. chopped onions
½ T. Worcestershire sauce
dash of pepper

Mix above ingredients and shape in form of a ball. Place in baking dish. Make a sauce of 1 can mushroom soup, 8 oz. cream cheese and ½ c. water. Pour over meatballs, after they have baked 20 min. in 375° oven. Sauce should be heated before adding. Serve over noodles or mashed potatoes.

Mushroom Hamburgers

1 lb. hamburgers

1 c. cracker crumbs

onions, salt, pepper and a little milk and make a roll - let stand overnight

Sauce:
1 can mushroom soup
3 T. ketchup
enough water to make sauce

1 chopped onion
2 T. Worcestershire sauce

Pour over hamburger and bake 50-60 min.

Pork Chop Casserole

6 lg. pork chops
milk and salt and pepper

1 lg. onion
1 med. head cabbage

Brown chops in a little butter or oleo. Turn and brown other side and slice on the onion. Put in large casserole. Shred cabbage fine and press over chops and onions. Pour enough milk over chops to barely cover. Add seasonings to taste. Bake covered for 55-60 min. at 350°. (We always serve this with baked potatoes, dipping some of the milk that's left in the bottom over them.)

Chipped Beef Casserole

¼ lb. chipped beef or dried beef or ham (cut fine)	1 can cream of mushroom soup
	¼ lb. Velveeta cheese
1 c. uncooked macaroni	1 c. milk
2 hard cooked eggs (diced)	2 T. grated onion

Mix together all ingredients. Pour into a 1½ to 2 qt. casserole. Let set for 6-12 hr. in refrigerator. Bake at 350° for ¾ hr. or until done. (We stir this while baking, as it get brown on top.)

Pork Chops Supreme

6-8 pork chops	1 can cream of chicken soup
½ c. water	

Dressing:

4 c. bread cubes	2 eggs
⅓ c. chopped celery	1 sm. onion, chopped
¼ c. melted butter	2 T. parsley flakes
salt and pepper to taste	

Brown pork chops and place in roaster. Make dressing by mixing all dressing ingredients together. Spoon dressing onto pork chops. Dilute soup with ½ c. water and pour over chops and dressing. Cover, bake in 350° oven for 1 hr.

Best Ever Salmon Loaf

2 c. canned salmon	1½ c. milk
2 c. bread crumbs	2 eggs beaten
1 tsp. salt	1½ T. parsley (minced)
1 T. melted butter	1 T. lemon juice

Flake salmon, add all ingredients. Mold into a loaf baking dish, buttered. Bake 40 min. at 375°. Serves 4.

Barbecued Liver

1 med. onion
2 T. oleo
½ lb liver, cut in
    ½" strips

2 T. vinegar
2 T. ketchup
1 tsp. salt
1 T. Worcestershire sauce

In a skillet, sauté onion in oleo until golden brown. Add liver and sauté until red disappears from liver. Add remaining ingredients. Cover and simmer until liver is tender. Even if you don't like liver you will like it this way. I use this recipe for deer liver.

Gala Ham Casserole

1 lb. ground ham
½ lb. ground pork
1½ lb. ground beef
salt and pepper

2 eggs (beaten)
1 c. cracker crumbs
1 c. milk

Mix the above ingredients together. Shape into loaf and place in baking dish or roasting pan. Make a glaze out of 1 c. brown sugar, 1 tsp. mustard, ⅓ c. vinegar, ½ c. water. Mix all together and cook about 5 min. Pour over the ham loaf and bake for 1½ hr. covered with ½ hr. uncovered at 350°.

Cheese Sausage Casserole

6 med. potatoes
    (cooked and sliced)
1 c. sour cream
1 sm. jar Cheese Whiz

2 T. chopped onion
1 T. parsley flakes
1 lb. package smokey
    links or smoked sausage

While potatoes are cooking, cut links in slices and blend other ingredients until smooth. Add links to sauce and add drained potatoes. Bake at 350° until bubbly and browning around edge. (This recipe is a bit expensive to make, but it's good and good reheated. May be stretched by adding milk or cream and more potatoes.)

Brick Cheese Lasagna

2 lb. hamburger
1 onion (chopped fine)
1 can tomato paste (12 oz.)
1½ c. water

½ lb. lasagna noodles
3 eggs
1 lb. cottage cheese
1 lb. brick cheese (sliced)

Brown hamburger and onion, add salt and pepper to taste. Add tomato sauce and water. Simmer 5 min. Cook and drain noodles. Beat eggs and add cottage cheese. Mix well. In a 9" x 13" pan, put a thin layer of meat sauce. Then a layer of half of the noodles, all of the cottage cheese mixture and half of the brick cheese. Next layer, half of remaining meat sauce. Add rest of the noodles, then remaining meat sauce. Top with brick cheese. Bake at 350° for ½ hr.

Party Ham Casserole

2 c. cut up ham
2 c. milk
1 can cream of celery soup
¼ c. onions (chopped)
½ tsp. salt

2 c. uncooked noodles (broken up slightly)
1 can cream of mushroom soup
2 c. Cracker Barrel cheese (grated)
1 can mushrooms (optional)

Mix ingredients and place in greased 9" x 13" pan. Cover and refrigerate overnight. Bake for about 45 min. at 350° until bubbly. You might want to try chicken in place of ham.

Dan's Hamburger Casserole

1 lb. hamburger
¼ lb. macaroni
2 tsp. salt
1 c. corn

2 med.-sized onions, minced
1½ qt. boiling water
¼ tsp. pepper
2 c. tomato juice

Mix chopped onion, ½ tsp. salt and pepper with hamburger. Cook macaroni in salt water until tender. Add corn, tomato juice and hamburger to the macaroni. Bake at 350° for 1 hr.

Pork Sausage Casserole

2 lb. bulk pork sausage
1 lb. can kidney beans
  (drain)
2 - 9 oz. cans New England
  or Boston Baked
  Beans
½ c. molasses
1 lb. can pork and beans

8½ oz. can pineapple (crushed and drained)
1 lb. can lima beans (drain)
½ c. minced onion
½ c. catsup
1 med. apple (shredded)
½ c. catsup
1 T. lemon juice
1 c. grated cheddar cheese

Brown sausage in skillet, drain. Place sausage in greased 3 qt. baking dish or roasting pan. Add beans, pineapple, onions, apple, molasses, catsup, and lemon juice. Toss, cover and bake at 300° for 2 hr. Remove cover, sprinkle with cheese and bake 30 min. uncovered.

Noodle Pizza Casserole

Melt in a med. saucepan ½ c. oleo. Blend until smooth 2 T. flour. Add, then cook until thickened, 2 c. milk. Remove from heat; then blend in and stir until smooth ¼ lb. Velveeta cheese.

Fold together:
1 lb. noodles, cooked and drained
2 lb. ground beef, browned and drained
4 c. spaghetti sauce   1 can mushroom soup

Put mixture in baking dish; then top with pepperoni slices. Bake at 350° for 30-45 min. Remove from oven and top with cheese. Return to oven until cheese is melted.

Cheesy Tuna Casserole

¼ c. chopped onions
1 can cream of
  mushroom soup
1 c. shredded cheese
1 - 8 oz. can tuna

2 T. margarine
½ c. milk
4 c. cooked macaroni
buttered bread crumbs

In med. saucepan, cook onion in margarine until tender. Stir in soup, milk, ¾ c. of cheese, macaroni and tuna. Pour in baking dish. Bake at 250° for 25 min. Top with bread crumbs and remaining cheese. Bake 5 more min.

Sharp Cheese Supper Dish

9 slices bread (buttered
    and cubed)
2 c. milk
3 eggs (beaten)

1 tsp. salt
1 tsp. dry mustard dissolved in a little water
2 c. sharp cheese (grated)

Mix the bread, milk and beaten eggs along with dry mustard and cheese. Pour into glass baking dish. Let set for 20 min. Bake about 30 min. at 375°.

Pot Luck Casserole

2 lb. jacket boiled
    potatoes, peeled
    and chopped
½ stick melted butter
1 can cream of chicken
    soup (undiluted)
2 c. corn flakes (crushed)
    and mixed with
    ¼ c. butter

¼ tsp. pepper
½ c. chopped onion
1 tsp. salt
1 pt. sweet cream
2 c. grated sharp cheddar cheese

Combine potatoes with ½ stick melted butter in large mixing bowl. Add salt, pepper, onion, soup, sweet cream and cheese. Blend thoroughly. Pour into greased casserole and cover with crushed corn flakes mixed with butter. Bake until golden brown at 350°.

Stuffing Mix Casserole

2 lb. zucchini
2 carrots, grated
½ c. sour cream
1 pkg. Kellogg's Croquettes
    Stuffing Mix

1 can cream of chicken soup
½ c. melted butter
salt and pepper to taste

Boil squash that has been cut into pieces and cook until tender, about 15 min. Drain well. Mix cooked squash, soup, carrots, sour cream and seasonings. Put in buttered casserole, cover with stuffing and pour melted butter over stuffing. Bake about 30-35 min. in 350° oven. When it's brown and bubbly, it's done.

Chicken Pot Pie

1 broiler chicken, cook until soft, then take meat from broth and cut up fine. Cut potatoes in cubes and cook along with meat. Some people just use potatoes instead of meat. Then add butter. Make dough of sweet cream, work in flour until real stiff. Roll out and cut in squares. Cook for 15 min. or more. If broth is not salty add salt to dough.

Pot Pie:

8 T. flour	2 eggs
1½ tsp. baking powder	sweet milk to make a dough
a little salt	

Cook from 10 to 15 min.

Skillet Supper

1 lb. hamburger	1 c. water
4 med. potatoes	1½ tsp. salt
¾ c. pet milk or whole milk	pepper to taste
4 med. carrots	4 T. shortening
2 med. carrots	

Brown hamburger in skillet with shortening. Put vegetables through med. knife of food grinder. Add to hamburger with water, salt and pepper. Cover, cook slowly about 20 min. or until vegetables are tender. Stir occasionally. Add milk and cook uncovered until thick.

Casserole for Rabbit

2 - 2½ lb. dressed rabbit	1 egg slightly beaten
1½ tsp. salt	½ c. dry bread crumbs or
¼ tsp. pepper	cracker crumbs

Turn oven to 400°. Grease 2 qt. casserole. Cut rabbit into serving pieces. Add seasoning to beaten egg. Dip each piece of rabbit in the egg mixture, then into the crumbs. Put in casserole, cover and bake 1 hr. or until tender and nicely browned. Uncover and serve at once.

Mother's Casserole

2 lb. hamburger
¾ c. celery (chopped)
1 c. onion (chopped)
½ c. uncooked rice

1 can mushroom soup
1 can cream of chicken soup
2½ c. water
2 tsp. Worcestershire sauce

Brown meat in skillet, stir to crumble and then drain. Put in a greased casserole dish, add all other ingredients. Bake 2 hr. at 250°.

Two-Cheese Casserole

2 c. uncooked noodles
1 lb. hamburger
1 c. milk
1 egg
1 c. grated cheddar cheese

1 T. salt
1 T. diced onions
1 can cream of mushroom soup
1 c. cottage cheese

Fry hamburger and onion until it changes color, mix in cottage cheese. Set aside until noodles are half tender. Put noodles, hamburger in layers in casserole starting and ending with noodles. Mix soup and milk, pour over mixture. Beat egg and pour over soup mixture. Sprinkle with cheese on top. Bake at 350° for 1 hr.

Good 'N Easy Casserole

2 lb. of fried hamburg, enough mashed potatoes to cover hamburg, 1 qt. beans and 1 can mushroom soup. Put in layers in loaf pan and bake for 15 min. in 350° oven. You may want to serve applesauce or tossed salad with it.

Ruth's Rice Casserole

1 lb. hamburger (brown it)
1 onion (brown it)
½ c. raw rice

1 can mushroom soup
1 can chicken soup
2 c. water

Mix all ingredients and bake 1½ hr. at 350°. Stir several times while baking.

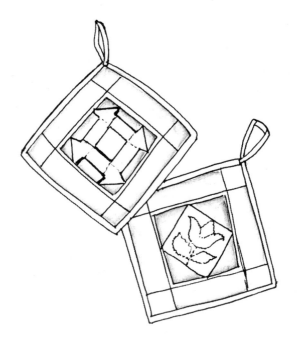

Soups, Sandwiches, and Pizza

Suppertime

My favorite meal of the day was suppertime, because that was the only meal my schoolteacher sister ate with us, and it was our biggest meal. Mother hardly ever made casseroles—she made mashed potatoes, meat and gravy, homemade noodles, garden vegetables and greens and crusty homemade bread. After we were done eating, we stayed to visit awhile before we went back to work. Sister always had some amusing or hilarious incidents to relate from her school day (and sometimes some not so amusing). Sometimes Dad or Mother had stories to tell from their younger days, or *rumshpringing* stories. Precious memories.

One not-so-precious memory comes to my mind, too. We were all sitting at the supper table visiting, talking and laughing, when there came a knock at the door. It was our English neighbor man—he looked very sad and told us that he had accidentally hit and killed our beloved farm dog with his truck. Oh no, not Taffy, our big, friendly, faithful Shepherd mix! Apparently he had been chasing a cat across the road. Dad assured the man that it wasn't his fault, but he still felt badly. The next day his wife stopped in and said she wanted to bring our supper over that evening. Mother tried to persuade her that they didn't owe us anything, but she insisted that we had done far more for them than they had ever done for us, and that she wanted to do this much for us. That evening we had different fare than we usually did—hamburgers, French fries, corn chips, milkshakes, orange soda, and a big, decorated bakery cake. It was good, but we all agreed that we wouldn't want it all the time—our usual home-cooked meals hit the spot better (and we slept better on it, too).

Bacon Lentil Soup

1½ c. lentils, rinsed and
    drained
6 c. water
2 slices bacon, diced
½ tsp. oregano
1 - 1 lb. can whole tomatoes
2 stalks celery with tops,
    sliced

1 clove garlic, minced
1½ tsp. salt
¼ tsp. pepper
1 med. onion, chopped
2 carrots, thinly sliced
2 T. lemon juice

Mix all ingredients together in a crock pot and cook on low for 8 to 9 hr.
Makes 2 qt.

Cheddar Mushroom Soup

3 c. water
3 bouillon cubes
4 med. potatoes,
    peeled and diced
1 med. onion, sliced
½ bunch broccoli,
    finely chopped

½ lb. sliced mushrooms, optional
⅓ c. margarine
⅓ c. flour
3½ c. milk or half and half
4 c. (1 lb.) shredded sharp
    cheddar cheese
½ c. diced green pepper, optional

Combine water and bouillon in Dutch oven. Bring to boil. Add vegetables
and simmer till tender. Melt butter in heavy saucepan; blend in flour and cook
1 min. Gradually add milk. Cook over med. heat until thickened, stirring
constantly. Add cheese; stir till melted. Stir cheese sauce into vegetable
mixture. Cook until heated over low heat. Do not boil Serves 8 to 10.

Chili and Macaroni Soup

1 qt. tomatoes
1 qt. kidney beans
1 lg. onion (chopped)

1 qt. hamburger
2 c. macaroni
1 tsp. chili powder

Cook macaroni and beans. Fry onions good and brown. Chop hamburger
and add all together and heat. Add salt and brown sugar to taste. Seal in jars
and pressure cook ½ hr. at 10 lb.

Barley Vegetable Soup

2 qt. beef and broth
1 qt. tomatoes
1½ c. barley
1 c. carrots
1 c. potatoes
1 c. celery

½ c. onion
¼ c. parsley
½ tsp. thyme
1 tsp. basil
salt and pepper to taste

Cook together till barley is soft. Stir once in awhile as barley thickens. Good for crock pot.

Chicken Noodle Soup to Can

1 gal. diced potatoes
1 gal. diced carrots
8 chickens, cooked
    and diced

1 gal. diced celery
1 gal. fine noodles
parsley, salt and pepper to taste

Boil each vegetable separately till half done. Save water from vegetables for juice. Add water if too thick. Add 4 boxes Lipton noodle soup. Cold pack 2½ - 3 hr.

Broccoli Carrot Soup

1 - 10 oz. frozen
    broccoli or
    2½ c. fresh
½ c. grated carrots
2 chicken bouillion cubes

1 qt. half cream and half water
½ lb. Velveeta
½ c. flour
¼ c. butter

Cook broccoli and carrots; add cream and flour. Best if shaken together. Add remaining ingredients, stir until melted. Great with crackers and sandwiches.

Cheddar Broccoli Soup

1 - 10 oz. frozen broccoli
    or 2½ c. fresh
1 qt. light cream
½ c. chopped celery

½ c. flour
¼ c. butter
2 chicken bouillon cubes
½ lb. cheddar cheese

Cook broccoli and celery and add cream and flour. Best if shaken together. Add remaining ingredients, stir until melted. Great with crackers and sandwiches.

Potato Cheese Soup

2 c. water
2 c. cubed potatoes
½ c. carrots, chopped
    or grated
½ c. celery, diced
¼ tsp. pepper

1 c. meat (bacon, tuna, salmon,
    sausage, hamburger, etc.)
2 c. grated cheese
1½ tsp. salt
¼ c. onion, diced

White Sauce:
¼ c. butter
¼ c. flour
2 c. milk

Cook together first 7 ingredients till vegetables are tender. Don't drain. Meanwhile, fry meat if using hamburger, sausage or bacon. Drain. In saucepan, melt butter and stir in flour. Cook together, then add milk and cook till thick. Stir this mixture, meat and cheese into cooked vegetables. Heat. Serve piping hot. Serves 6. We really like this made with tuna.

VARIATION: If using bacon, omit ¼ c. butter in white sauce. Use 2 T. bacon drippings and 2 T. butter instead. This gives the chowder an excellent flavor.

Minestrone Soup

1 lb. ground beef
1 c. cubed raw potatoes
½ c. diced celery
1-2 cans tomatoes
1 sm. can peas
½ tsp. thyme
4 tsp. salt
1½ qt. water

1 c. diced onion
1 c. sliced carrots
1 c. shredded cabbage
¼ c. rice
bay leaf crushed
1 basil leaf
⅛ tsp. pepper

Brown ground beef and onion in a lg. pan. Add next five ingredients, bring to a boil. Sprinkle rice into mixture. Add remaining ingredients, cover and simmer 1 hr. Serve as a main dish topped with shredded cheese. Serves 6.

Chili Soup to Can

Brown together:
5 lb. hamburger	2 T. salt
3 c. onions, chopped	1 T. pepper

Add:
2 qt. can tomato juice	1 can water
2 c. ketchup	½ gal. kidney beans
1½ tsp. chili powder	1 T. salt

Put in jars and cold pack 2 hr.

Turkey Vegetable Soup

1 lb. ground turkey	1 c. diced onion
1 c. cubed raw potatoes	1 c. sliced carrots
½ c. diced celery	1 c. shredded cabbage
1-2 cans tomatoes	¼ c. rice
1 sm. bunch parsley	bay leaf, crushed
½ tsp. thyme	1 basil leaf
4 tsp. salt	⅛ tsp. pepper
1½ qt. water	

Brown ground turkey and onion in a lg. pan. Add next five ingredients, bring to a boil. Sprinkle rice into mixture. Add remaining ingredients, cover and simmer 1 hr. Serve as a main dish, topped with shredded cheese. Serves 6.

White Bean Soup

2 T. butter	1 - 20 oz. can white beans, drained
½ c. finely chopped celery	2 tsp. Worcestershire sauce
1 lg. carrot, chopped	⅛ tsp. red pepper
1 c. chopped onion	½ tsp. salt
2 c. diced potatoes	1½ c. shredded cheddar cheese
2 c. water	1 c. milk

In large saucepot, melt butter. Add celery, carrots and onions. Cook over med. heat, stirring frequently, until vegetables are tender, about 15 min. Add potatoes, water, beans, Worcestershire, pepper and salt. Bring to a boil. Reduce heat and simmer 45 min. Remove from heat. Stir in cheese and milk. Makes 6 c.

Ham and Cheddar Soup

2 c. water
½ c. diced carrots
¼ c. chopped onion
¼ tsp. pepper

2 c. diced potatoes
½ c. diced celery
1 tsp. salt

White Sauce:
¼ c. butter
2 c. milk
1 c. cubed ham

¼ c. flour
2 c. cheddar cheese, grated

Combine water, vegetables and seasonings in large kettle. Boil 10 min. In sm. saucepan, make white sauce by melting butter, add flour, stir till smooth. Slowly add milk; add white sauce, cheese and ham to vegetables that have not been drained. Heat thoroughly. Serve with crackers.

Beef Vegetable Chowder

2½ gal. water
2 lg. cans beef
1 c. each white
   and brown sugar

1¼ c. beef soup mix
4 qt. tomato juice
1 stick butter
¼ c. salt

Take approx. 2 qt. flour and add water to make a smooth paste to thicken soup; heat to boiling point, then mix in vegetables which have been cooked and salted separate.

4 qt. carrots, cut up fine
4 qt. peas
4 qt. hamburger
   or chunk beef

4 qt. potatoes, cut in sm. pieces
2 lg. onions

Brown hamburger and onions together. Makes 21 qt. Cold pack 2 hr.

Creamed Mushroom Soup

Pick and clean any good variety of mushrooms. Chop 2 c. of mushrooms and add 7 heaping T. flour in 1 c. oleo or butter. Brown, then add some cold water and milk to desired thickness. Add salt and pepper to suit taste. Makes approximately 6 qt.

Carla's Chili Soup

4 lb. hamburger
    (fry in butter)
1 qt. red kidney beans
2 red peppers

3 qt. strained tomatoes
chili powder to taste
12 sm. onions

Cook each separate, then mix and cook ½ hr.

Tomato Soup (to can)

6 onions
1 bunch celery
8 qt. fresh tomatoes
1 c. sugar

¼ c. salt
1 c. butter
1 c. flour

Cook tomatoes, onions and chopped celery until tender. Put through strainer and then put juice back in kettle and add sugar and salt. Cream butter and flour and add to juice. Blend well and boil until slightly thickened, stirring all the time. Put boiling soup in jars and seal. Makes 12 pt. Process in hot water bath for 10 min.

Fresh Tomato Soup

6 med. sized tomatoes
1 onion, chopped
1 stalk celery, chopped
1 T. tomato paste
½ tsp. salt

½ tsp. dried basil
¼ tsp. black pepper
2 c. chicken broth
½ c. yogurt

Cut tomatoes into wedges and place in 1½ qt. saucepan with all ingredients except yogurt. Simmer uncovered for 30 min. Strain to remove tomato seeds and skins. Adjust seasonings to taste and garnish with spoonfuls of yogurt.

Cubed Beef Soup

4 qt. carrots
4 qt. potatoes
3 qt. peas

2 qt. green beans
2 lg. onions
1 qt. cooked alphabets

Cut up and cook vegetables until partly soft. Cook alphabets until soft. Mix together. Can add tomato juice.

Chicken Rivvel Soup

Chicken Broth:
1 fryer chicken,
    2½ lb. cut up

6 c. cold water
3 chicken bouillon cubes

Soup Base:
1 can chicken
    broth (10¾ oz.)
1 c. chopped celery
¼ c. chopped onions
1 c. fresh or frozen peas

1 can cream of chicken soup (10¾ oz.)
1 can cream of mushroom soup (10¾ oz.)
1½ c. chopped carrot
1 c. chopped potatoes

Cook fryer, cut in pieces, reserved chicken broth and 1 tsp. seasoned salt

Rivvels:
2 c. flour
¼ tsp. pepper
1 egg
⅔ c. milk

1 tsp. salt
4 tsp. baking powder
2 T. butter

Place fryer, water and bouillon in kettle and bring to boil. Let simmer until chicken is tender. Cut up chicken in bite size pieces and set aside. Strain chicken broth. Put chicken and broth in large kettle, add rest of soup base ingredients, simmer soup on low heat until vegetables are tender. Mix up rivvels by sifting dry ingredients together. Add butter, egg, and milk to make stiff batter. Drop by tsp. into boiling liquid. Cook covered and without "peeking" for 20 min.

Ham and Bean Soup

1 lb. navy beans,
    soak overnight
3 qt. water
2 c. potatoes, shredded
1 qt. ham, finely chopped

½ c. onions, chopped
1 qt. tomato juice
4 tsp. salt
2 c. celery, finely chopped
1 c. carrots, shredded

Bring water and beans to a boil. Boil until soft. Add vegetables and meat. Add tomato juice and bring to a boil. Put in sterile jars, then in hot water bath for 2 hr. This tastes like bought Ham-N-Bean soup.

Vera's Vegetable Soup

1 qt. potatoes
1 qt. corn
1 qt. carrots
1 qt. peas
1 qt. onions

1 qt. celery
1 qt. navy beans
1 qt. alphabets
7 qt. tomato juice
3 lb. hamburger

Cook each one separate and add to boiling tomato juice. Add 1 tsp. chili powder, 1 tsp. pepper, 1 c. brown sugar, and salt to taste. Fill jars to neck and then put in hot water bath for 3 hr.

Spinach Soup

1 tsp. butter
1½ c. onion, chopped
1 qt. spinach, pureed
½ tsp. garlic powder
1 tsp. salt

½ tsp. celery salt
dash pepper
1 c. evaporated milk
1 pt. milk

In a saucepan, melt butter. Sauté onion and spinach. Combine rest of ingredients and add milk. Bring to boiling point. Serves 12 to 14. (To sauté, cook in butter until soft. To puree spinach, boil in a little water and then put through sieve and then add to onion.)

Bean 'N Bacon Soup

4 lb. dried navy beans,
    soaked overnight
    then cooked
4 c. carrots, diced
4 to 6 c. celery, diced
8 c. potatoes, diced

4 to 6 c. ham, cubed
2 tsp. black pepper
2 lb. bacon
6 c. onions, diced
2 bay leaves (optional)
salt to taste

Cook potatoes, carrots and celery until soft. Add ham and cook until ham is heated. Cut up bacon finely and fry. Remove bacon and cook onions in bacon grease until soft. Put all ingredients together in canner and heat until it simmers. Remove bay leaves before putting in jars. Process 2 hr. in hot water bath. Makes about 16 qt.

Super Spaghetti Soup

3 lb. spaghetti, cooked soft
3 qt. celery, cooked soft
¼ lb. butter

1 qt. carrots, cooked soft
4 lb. hamburger
1 c. onions, cut fine

Fry hamburger, onions and butter together for 30 min.

Sauce:
(The sauce may be made the day before and put into cold storage.)

1 basket (½ bu.) tomatoes
2 stalks celery
12 onions
1 tsp. pepper

1 c. vinegar
¼ lb. butter
1 tsp. celery seed

Cook all these ingredients together for approximately 30 min. or until celery and onions are soft. Then put through your food processor. Mix vegetables, spaghetti, meat and sauce together in one big tub. Fill qt. jars and then put in hot water bath for 2 hr. Quick wintertime meal.

Potato Soup and Dumplings

1 c. diced celery. Put in 4 qt. pot with 1 c. water. Cook until just tender, do not drain. Peel and cube 6 med. potatoes, put in with cooked celery and add 1½ c. water. Add one med. onion chopped fine, 1 tsp. salt and ¼ tsp. pepper. Cook until potatoes are tender. Mash all slightly to eliminate definite cubes. Add 3 c. milk. Set aside and prepare dumplings.

Dumplings:
1 c. sifted flour
½ tsp. sugar
1 egg, mixed with ½ c. milk

1½ tsp. baking powder
1 tsp. dry parsley flakes

Add liquid to dry ingredients until moistened. Drop by spoonfuls on boiling vegetables and milk. Cover and simmer about 10 min. or until dumplings are done.

Cream of Broccoli Soup

2 T. butter, melted and slowly stir in 2 T. flour. Cook over low heat for 3 min., stirring often. Set aside. Wash and trim 1 bunch broccoli, chop into ½" pieces. Sauté 1 sm. onion in 2 T. butter. Stir in broccoli and cook covered for 3 min. Stir in 1 qt. chicken broth and heat to simmer, then stir some of broth into butter flour. Mix till smooth, now stir into broccoli. Mix, cover and cook till broccoli is done, about 30 min. Remove from heat and mash broccoli with a potato masher. If you like, stir in ½ c. heavy cream (warm). Salt and pepper to taste. Asparagus or cauliflower can also be used instead of broccoli.

Celery Soup

2 stalks celery	2 T. butter
1 qt. water	1 T. minced parsley
1 qt. hot milk	½ c. cream
2 T. flour	

Dice celery, using a few leaves. Cook slowly for ¾ hr. in 1 qt. water. When tender, press through a puree sieve. Add hot milk. Blend butter, flour and a little bit of hot soup. Stir all together until smooth and thickened. Add parsley and cream. Can be served with soufflé balls.

Deluxe Vegetable-Bean Soup

1 pkg. (1 lb.) Great northern dry beans	½ c. oil
2½ qt. water	1 lg. onion (chopped)
2 cloves garlic, minced or garlic salt	1 c. carrots, diced sm.
1 c. tomato juice	1 c. celery (chopped sm.)
3 T. minced parsley	1 tsp. oregano
	2 tsp. salt
	½ tsp. basil

In large kettle, soak beans overnight (or bring beans to a boil and cook 2 min., remove from heat, cover and let stand 1 hr.). Bring beans to boil, reduce heat, cover and simmer 1½ hr., or until beans are almost tender, adding more water if necessary. Heat oil in heavy skillet. Sauté onions, celery, carrots, garlic and oregano for about 10 min., stirring constantly. Add to beans, stir in tomatoes, parsley, salt and basil. Cook 1 hr. longer or until all is tender. Makes 3 qt. Delicious!

Bacon Onion Soup

4 slices bacon
4 onions, sliced or diced
2 lg. potatoes, peeled
    and diced
¼ tsp. curry powder

½ c. water
1 tsp. salt
2 T. parsley (snipped)
chicken broth (13¾ oz.)
1 can evaporated milk (14½ oz.)

In a lg. pan, fry bacon until crisp. Reserve 2 T. of drippings; drain and crumble bacon. Cook onions in reserved drippings until tender. Add diced potatoes, chicken broth, water and curry. Cover and cook 10 min. or until potatoes are tender. Stir in evaporated milk, parsley and bacon. Heat and serve.

Macaroni Chili Soup

1⅓ lb. hamburger
⅓ c. diced peppers
⅓ c. diced onions
¼ tsp. chili powder
½ tsp. parsley flakes

2 lb. 8 oz. can kidney beans
1 lb. 14 oz. can pork 'n beans
3 c. cooked macaroni
1 qt. canned tomatoes
salt and pepper to taste

Fry hamburger with peppers, onions, chili powder and parsley till nice and brown. Add to rest of ingredients in large kettle and bring to boil. Ready to serve 10.

Rice Chicken Soup

4 lb. chicken
2 c. carrots, diced
2 c. celery, diced
1 lb. noodles
½ c. rice

1 c. potatoes, diced
½ c. onion, diced
1 qt. corn
salt and pepper, to taste

Cook chicken, then debone it and save the broth. Add water to make 1 gal. liquid. Boil potatoes, carrots and celery in broth until tender. Then add noodles, rice, onion and corn and simmer until done. Can be frozen for handy meals.

Broccoli Potato Soup

1 c. broccoli, chopped
4 c. potatoes, diced
3 eggs (optional)

¼ c. chicken broth mix or
   1 can cream of chicken soup
2 c. milk

Add water to broccoli and potatoes, bring to a boil. Add raw eggs and cook until vegetables are soft. Use potato masher and mash slightly. Add chicken mix and stir. Add milk and heat slowly.

Pea Soup

1 qt. peas, cooked
1 c. ham, cubed
½ c. ham broth

3 c. milk
1 tsp. salt
1 T. sugar

Bring to boiling and thicken with 1 T. cornstarch mixed with a bit of water.

Parslied Chicken Noodle Soup

12 lb. chicken,
   cooked tender
3 lb. noodles, crushed
1 lb. chicken base
   (use all your broth
   from cooking chicken)

½ gal. carrots, diced sm.
2 stalks celery, cut fine
1 lg. can chicken broth
½ gal. potatoes
1 qt. parsley

Cook the chicken in water until tender (approximately 1½ hr.) with 1 T. salt. Save the broth and pick off the meat from bones. Cook the noodles and vegetables until soft, each in a separate pot. Then mix all ingredients together. Ready to eat or put in jars and hot water bath for 2½ hr.

Sunday Bean Soup

1 c. navy beans
1 ham bone or
   piece of ham
2 qt. boiling water
1 tsp. salt

2 c. carrots, diced
2 onions, diced
2 potatoes, diced
⅛ tsp. pepper

Add all ingredients to boiling water. Cook slowly until beans are tender, about 2 hr. Add more water if necessary. Remove bone.

Delicious Corn Soup

1½ c. corn
3 pt. milk
1 tsp. salt

1 T. sugar
2 eggs, well beaten
2 T. butter

Combine milk, corn, salt and sugar. Boil together for a few min. Add the well-beaten eggs (do not stir). Boil a little longer, then beat lightly. Add butter. Serve with crackers. This can be frozen, but is best made with frozen corn during winter months.

Wholesome Pizza Dough

1 pkg. dry yeast
½ c. warm water

2¼ c. whole grain mix (found
    in muffins and biscuits section)

Soften yeast in water. Stir in grain mix. Knead 25 strokes. Let rest 10 min. Pat out on a greased 14" pizza pan. Top as desired. Bake at 425° for 10 to 15 min.

Pizza Dough

1½ c. flour
¼ tsp. salt
1½ T. Wesson oil

½ T. yeast
½ c. water

Enough for 1 cookie sheet.

Easy Yorkshire Pizza

¼ c. butter
1 c. flour
¼ tsp. salt

2 eggs
1 c. milk

Melt butter in an 8" x 12" glass pan in 425° oven. Beat flour, eggs, milk, salt until smooth. Pour into hot pan. Put pizza sauce on, then other pizza toppings. Sprinkle with oregano and top with cheese. Bake at 400° for 15 to 20 min.

Easy Variety Pizza

In a bowl combine:

4 c. flour   6 tsp. baking powder
1 tsp. salt

Combine:

1⅓ c. milk   ⅔ c. Wesson oil

Pour all at once over flour mixture. Mix with fork then shape into ball. Knead until smooth. Roll out for about three 12" sheets. Place on greased cookie sheets.

Pizza Sauce:

Cmbine:

⅔ c. water   4 - 6 oz. cans tomato paste
⅔ c. Wesson oil   2 tsp. oregano
2 tsp. garlic powder   1 tsp. salt
½ tsp. pepper

Put on top of dough. Add hamburger, cheese or sausage, onions or green peppers. Bake at 400° for 20-25 min. Tomato juice may be thickened and used as a substitute for tomato paste.

Vegetable Pizza

Favorite pizza crust, baked and cooled.

2 - 8 oz. pkg. cream cheese	Carrots
1 pkg. Hidden Valley Ranch	Celery
dressing mix	Onion
1 c. salad dressing	Lettuce
Cauliflower	Cheese
Broccoli	

Mix first 3 ingredients and spread on crust. Top with any or all of the vegetables. Sprinkle with shredded cheese.

Deep Dish Pizza

3 c. Bisquick baking mix
    (or baking mix
    found in biscuits
    and muffins)
¾ c. water
1 lb. ground beef
8 oz. (2 c.) mozzarella
    cheese, shredded

2 cloves garlic, crushed
15 oz. can tomato sauce
1 tsp. Italian seasoning
4½ oz. jar sliced mushrooms, drained
½ c. green peppers, chopped
½ c. onion, chopped
½ tsp. salt

Mix baking mix and water. Knead 20 times on a floured surface. Pat dough on the bottom and up sides of a 10" x 5" lightly greased pan. Or put on a cookie sheet and build up edges. Brown beef and onion, salt and garlic; drain. Mix tomato sauce and Italian seasoning and spread over dough. Spoon beef mixture evenly over sauce. Top with mushrooms, green peppers and cheese. Bake in a preheated 425° oven approximately 20 min. Makes 8 servings.

Homemade Pizza

Crust:

1 pkg. dry yeast
1 c. warm water
1 tsp. sugar

1 tsp. salt
2 T. vegetable oil
2½ c. flour

Sauce:

8 oz. tomato paste
1 tsp. seasoned salt
1 tsp. oregano

1 tsp. Italian seasoning
⅛ tsp. garlic powder
dash of pepper

Topping:

1 T. dehydrated
    minced onion
1 T. dehydrated
    green pepper
4 oz. mushrooms

1 lb. sausage, browned and
    crumbled
4 oz. sliced pepperoni
8 oz. mozzarella cheese

Dissolve yeast in water; add sugar, salt and oil. Add flour and mix well. Cover and let rise in a warm place, about 5 min. Mix sauce and prepare toppings. Grease pan; flour fingers and spread crust. Pour on sauce, then other selected toppings. Bake at 425° for 18 to 20 min.

Pizza Sauce

3 qt. tomato juice
½ tsp. pepper
2 tsp. celery seed
1 tsp. cinnamon
½ c. chopped onions

2 T. salt
1 c. vinegar
¼ tsp. cloves
1 T. dry mustard
1½ c. sugar

Boil 30 min. and thicken with clear jell.

Pizza Sauce

1 qt. tomato juice
2 tsp. oregano
2 scant tsp. garlic powder
2 tsp. salt
1 tsp. pepper

½ c. onions, chopped
⅓ tsp. cloves
⅓ tsp. sweet basil
Sprinkle of brown sugar
1 heaping T. cornstarch

Boil together and sprinkle with cornstarch. Boil about ½ hr. or a little more.

Velveeta Burgers

1½ lb. hamburger
1 sm. box Velveeta cheese

1 sm. onion
1 can cream of mushroom soup

Brown hamburger and onion till brown. Add soup and cheese. Stir till melted. Serve on hamburger buns.

Weiner Burgers

8 hot dogs, diced
1 c. diced cheese
1 T. mustard

1 T. catsup
1 T. onion
1 T. chopped pickles

Mix all ingredients and fill wiener buns. Wrap in foil and bake 15 min. at 325° or longer.

The beauty of a home is harmony,
The joy of a home is love.
The security of a home is loyalty
To each other and to God above.

Barbecue Sandwiches

1 lb. ham	1 tsp. mustard
1 c. ketchup	½ tsp. paprika
3 T. brown sugar	¼ c. water
2 T. dark jelly	

Boil together and put in hamburger buns. (I like to use the crock pot to boil it.)

Egg Salad Sandwiches

3 hard-cooked eggs, chopped	1 T. mayonnaise or salad dressing
1 T. onion, finely chopped	2 tsp. pickle relish
½ tsp. salt	

Combine all ingredients. Mix well. Makes 1 c. Spread on bread.

Favorite Sandwiches

Put in top of double boiler:

2 lb. hamburger	1 c. catsup
2 onions (diced)	1 tsp. prepared mustard
1 tsp. chili	salt to taste

Cook 1 hr. Serve hot for sandwiches or bread or buns.

Chipped Ham Sandwiches

1 lb. chipped ham or	1 sm. onion, diced fine (opt.)
1 lb. chipped or	½ c. catsup
thinly sliced bologna	1-3 T. brown sugar
1 T. mustard	

Combine above ingredients. Place a layer of meat, then a layer of sauce in a casserole, finished with sauce on top. Bake at 300° for 1 hr. or instead of baking, add ½ c. water to sauce and cook everything but meat on top of stove for 20 min., add meat and heat thoroughly until done. Toss it with a fork instead of a spoon while stirring.

Hot Chicken Sandwiches

½ lb. chopped chicken
½ lb. chopped cheese
⅓ c. chopped onion
2 hard-boiled eggs

½ c. pickle relish or chopped olives
3 T. mayonnaise
½ c. chili sauce or ketchup
12 buns

Mix all ingredients together. Fill buns. Wrap in foil. Bake 10 to 20 min. until thoroughly heated.

Beef-Cheese Sandwiches

8 slices bread, lightly toasted
Prepared mustard
8 thin slices beef, cooked
    or roasted
12 slices cheese
Pimento, optional
Fresh parsley sprigs, optional

Dressing:
¾ c. mayonnaise
2 tsp. horseradish
⅓ c. pickle radish
½ tsp. Worcestershire sauce

Cover broiler grid with foil, shinny side up. Completely spread 1 side of lightly toasted bread slices with mustard. Place on broiler grid, mustard side up. Put beef on bread, then cheese. Combine dressing ingredients and mix well. Spread over each sandwich to within ½" of the edge. I put the cheese slice on top. Broil 3" to 4" from heat until dressing bubbles.

Turkey Sandwiches

2 c. cooked, diced turkey
½ c. diced celery
½ c. diced cheddar cheese
1 tsp. pimento
2 hard-boiled eggs, chopped

2 T. chopped onion or chives
½ c. mayonnaise
salt and pepper
6 hamburger buns

Combine all ingredients, except buns. Butter tops of buns and fill. Wrap in foil. Heat in 400° oven for 15 to 20 min. These are good cold, too. Or if you're in a hurry, heat filling mixture in microwave, then fill buns.

Sloppy Joes

2½ lb. hamburger
1 med. onion, chopped
2½ T. Worcestershire sauce
½ c. ketchup
1 - 10¾ oz. can cream
    of mushroom soup

⅓ c. brown sugar
1 T. prepared mustard
salt
pepper

Fry hamburger and onion. Sprinkle with salt and pepper. Drain. Add Worcestershire sauce, ketchup, soup, sugar and mustard. Heat and serve on warm buns.

Tasty Tuna Sandwiches

7 oz. can tuna
2 hard-boiled eggs
½ c. mayonnaise
¼ lb. cheese
2 T. green pepper

2 T. chopped onion
2 T. pickles
2 T. olives
hamburger buns

Mix together everything but the buns. Spread on buns and wrap in foil. Bake at 250° for 30 min. Makes 8.

Gourmet Goulash

1½-2 lb. round stead,
    cut in 1½" cubes
1 lg. onion (sliced)
1 - 16 oz. stewed
    tomatoes (undrained)
1 bay leaf
1 tsp. sugar
Hot cooked noodles
¼ tsp. pepper

2-3 T. flour
3 T. vegetable oil
1 clove garlic (chopped fine)
2 tsp. paprika
2 tsp. Wyler's beef flavor
    (instant bouillon)
1 tsp. thyme
8 oz. container sour cream

Coat meat with flour, in large skillet brown meat in oil. Pour off fat and add onion and garlic. Cook until tender. Add remaining ingredients, except noodles and sour cream. Cover and simmer 1 hr. and 30 min. or until meat is tender. Remove from heat and uncover. After 5 min. stir about ¼ c. sauce into sour cream. Add slowly to mixture in skillet. Stir constantly until sour cream is blended. Do not boil. Serve this over cooked noodles. Serves 6-8 people.

Busy-day Stew

1 lb. hamburger
1 c. diced carrots
2 c. tomato juice
1½ tsp. salt

1 c. chopped onions
½ c. green peppers (opt.)
1 c. diced potatoes
⅛ tsp. pepper

Fry hamburger and onions together. Have carrots, potatoes and celery cooked; then combine this all together and heat and serve with crackers.

Beef and Sauerkraut Supper

1½ lb. lean beef with visible
    fat removed
    (cubed 1½")
2 sm. onions, quartered
½ tsp. paprika

¼ tsp. salt
½ tsp. black pepper
1 bay leaf
1 c. boiling water
¾ lb. sauerkraut

Brown meat and onions in pan, sprayed with non-stick spray. Season with salt, pepper and paprika. Add half of water. Cook over low heat for ½ hr. Stir in sauerkraut, cover and cook 10 min. Add bay leaf and rest of water. Cover and cook 1½ hr. Remove bay leaf before serving. Yield: six 1 c. servings.

One-Dish Meal

9 slices bacon
3 onions, chopped
2 cans peas
2 lb. spaghetti, cooked
2 cans mushroom soup
1½-2 qt. tomato soup

3 lb. hamburger
3 c. carrots, cut and cooked
1 c. celery, cut and cooked
3 c. diced potatoes, cooked
1 lb. Velveeta cheese

Fry bacon; take out. Heat hamburger and onions in bacon grease. Put in roaster. Add potatoes, carrot, celery, peas, spaghetti and mushroom soup. Then arrange cheese slices and bacon on top. Pour tomato soup over all. Bake in moderate oven, 350-375° for 1½-2 hr.

Washday Stew

1 lb. stewing meat
4 lg. potatoes
   (cut in chunks)

4 med. carrots (cut in chunks)
1 c. celery (cut in sm. pieces)
1 sm. onion

Put meat in bottom of casserole (raw) and add raw vegetables. Sprinkle on top: 1 tsp. salt, ⅛ tsp. pepper and 2 T. Minute Tapioca. Pour on top: 1 - 10 oz. can tomato soup or juice, 1 - 10 oz. can water. (Homemade tomato soup works fine, but if you use tomato juice, add 1 tsp. sugar.) Cover and bake 5 hr. at 275°, or bake at 375° for 30 min., then turn down to 300° for remainder of time (2½ more hr.). Vegetables, meat and gravy should all be a rich brown when done. If you trust your oven temp., don't lift lid till done.

Sylvia's Stromboli

1 T. yeast
1 tsp. sugar
2 T. oil

1 c. warm water
1 tsp. salt
2½ c. bread flour

Mix like bread dough and leave set for 5 min. Roll out into 6 parts and fill with meat, cheese, and onions. Fold together and seal edges. Bake 20 min. at 400°.

Midwestern Beef Stew

3 T. flour
1 tsp. salt
½ tsp. celery salt
¼ tsp. garlic salt
¼ tsp. pepper
½ tsp. ginger
3 lb. chuck, cut in 2" cubes

2 T. shortening or bacon fat
1 - 1 lb. can whole tomatoes
3 med. onions, sliced
⅓ c. red wine vinegar
½ c. molasses
¾ c. water
½ c. raisins

6 carrots, cut diagonal (1" pieces), 6 potatoes, pared and quartered. Combine flour, salt, celery salt, garlic salt, pepper and ginger in sm. bowl. Toss beef cubes in mixture. Melt shortening in large Dutch oven over med. heat. Add beef cubes and brown. Add tomatoes, onion, vinegar, molasses and water. Bring to a boil over high heat; cover and simmer about 2 hr. Add carrots, raisins and potatoes; simmer 30 min. longer or until vegetables are tender. Thicken gravy with a mixture of ¼ c. flour and 3 T. water. Makes 8 servings.

Workman's Stew

Melt 1 T. shortening, add 1 lb. ground beef. Brown over med. heat. Add 1 T. salt, 1 - 10½ oz. can tomato soup, 2 soup cans of water. Cover tightly and let cook slowly until tender. About 1 hr. Add 3 carrots cut up, 3 potatoes cut up and 2 onions cut up. Cover and continue cooking slowly about 30 min. If there is not enough liquid, add more water. If stew is too thin, remove lid and cook until thick.

Kidney Stew

2 lb. pork kidneys	1 bay leaf (optional)
1 clove garlic (chopped fine)	1 T. paprika
2 onions chopped	salt to taste
3 T. shortening	

Cut kidneys lengthwise, then crosswise. Cut away all white tissue. Soak several hr. in salt water, then rinse thoroughly in cold water. Fry onions till tender. Add kidneys and all other ingredients. Cover and simmer 2 hr. until meat is tender. Add warm water if liquid evaporates. Serve with whole boiled potatoes and carrots (cooked separately). Note: Since kidneys are such a mess to prepare, I double the recipe, which keeps well in refrigerator.

A Grandmother's Washday "Receet"

1. Bild fire in backyard to het kettle of rain water.
2. Set tubs so smoke won't blow in eyes if wind is peart.
3. Shave 1 hole cake lie sope in bilin water.
4. Sort things. Make 3 piles. 1 pile white. 1 pile cullard.
   1 pile werk britches and rags.
5. Stur flour in cold water to smooth, then thin down with bilin water.
6. Rub dirt spots on board. Scrub hard. Then bile. Rub cullard but
   don't bile, just rench and starch.
7. Take white things out of kettle with broomstick handle, then rench,
   blew and starch.
8. Spread tee towels on grass.
9. Hang old rags on fence.
10. Pour rench water on flower bed.
11. Scrub porch with hot sopy water.
12. Turn tubs upside down.
13. Go put on clean dress—smooth hair with side combs, brew cup of
    tea—set and rest and rock a spell and count blessin.

—Author Unknown

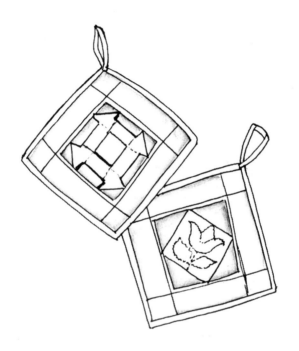

Salads and Pickles

The Working Bee

I always enjoyed the times we had workmen to feed, such as at silo-filling time or at threshing time. Mother surpassed herself then, in cooking, for the hard-working men needed plenty of good food to eat. She prepared crocks of pudding, gallons of fruit jam and plenty of stewed prunes. I helped her make angel food cakes, and cherry, raisin or grape pies. The pantry shelf was also stocked with many loaves of freshly baked bread, tightly wrapped in a clean tablecloth. Mounds of egg-rich yellow noodles had been prepared in advance, and enough saffron flowers gathered to flavor them. Several batches of doughnuts had been deep-fat fried and rolled into 10x sugar.

We would get up early in the morning to butcher as many chickens as we needed to feed the men. Mother easily beheaded her own chickens—she pounded two nails into a block of wood, then inserted the head between them, held the legs with one hand, and whacked the hatchet with the other.

There were mounds of potatoes to be peeled, and peas, lima beans or corn to be gathered from the garden for our vegetable, and a salad to prepare, although we didn't call it that, then. In addition to all these, Mother always made a fresh batch of cup cheese, and bought a big tin of hard pretzels from the pretzel man that stopped at our farm once a month.

I remember one busy forenoon when we were ready to peel the potatoes—we couldn't find the paring knives! (Unbeknownst to us, the boys had used them to scale fish the night before and left them lay by the woodpile.) Mother was quite flustered as we scurried around, hunting every place we could think of. Finally she gave up and quickly hitched old Pearl to the spring wagon and drove the mile to the neighbors to borrow one. I'm sure that placid old mare must have wondered what was going on—instead of being allowed to go at her usual leisurely pace, she was urged to go at a breakneck speed! It took a little more hectic rushing around, but, thankfully, dinner was ready when the men came filing in from the barn and field, and Mother's reputation was saved!

Easy Potato Salad

12 c. cooked, diced potatoes	12 eggs, hard-boiled
½ onion, chopped	2 c. celery, chopped
3 c. salad dressing	½ c. milk
6 T. mustard	2 tsp. salt
1½ c. white sugar	½ c. vinegar

Peel potatoes and eggs and chop. Add onions and celery. Mix other ingredients and pour over potato mixture. Toss. This is best made 2 or 3 days before serving. Makes 1 gal.

Tuna Macaroni Salad

1 lb. elbow macaroni, cooked and cooled	1 family size can tuna, drained
4 hard-boiled eggs, chopped	1 med. onion, minced
4 slices bacon, fried and crushed	2 stalks celery, chopped
	3 med. carrots, grated

Dressing:

2½ c. mayonnaise	2 T. vinegar
1 c. sugar	¾-1 c. milk
⅓ c. mustard	

Cook macaroni as directed on package until tender. Drain. Add the rest of the ingredients, flaking tuna as you add it. Then add the dressing which has been well blended. Serves 12-15.

Crunchy Vegetable Salad

2 c. broccoli floweretes	1 c. celery
2 c. cauliflueretes	1 c. cherry tomatoes (halved)
1 c. sliced zucchini	¾ c. sliced green onions
½ c. pitted ripe olives sliced	¼ c. carrots (sliced)
1 c. Italian dressing	1 jar Hormel bacon bits

In a lg. bowl, combine all ingredients except bacon. Cover, let marinate in refrigerator, turning occasionally, 4 hr. or overnight. Just before serving toss with bacon bits. Serves 8.

Best Broccoli Salad

1 bundle broccoli (cut fresh) in sm. pieces
1 med. onion, diced
2 c. grated cheese

Sauce:

1 c. sour cream   ½ tsp. salt
1 c. mayonnaise   ½ c. sugar

Mix sauce ingredients, then pour over broccoli mixture.

Jane's Macaroni Salad

2 c. dry macaroni   1½ c. celery, chopped
1 onion, chopped   1 tsp. parsley
1 carrot, grated   6 eggs, hard boiled
Celery seed to taste

Dressing:

1½ c. sugar   ¼ c. mustard
¼ c. flour   ¼ tsp. salt
1½ c. water   ½ c. vinegar (scant)
1 c. Miracle Whip

Cook macaroni as directed and drain. Mix with remaining salad ingredients. Cook together the first 5 ingredients. Cool. Add mustard and Miracle Whip. Stir into macaroni mixture.

Bacon Potato Salad

6 slices bacon   ½ c. chopped onions
2 T. flour   2 T. sugar
1½ tsp. salt   1 tsp. celery seed
dash of pepper   1 c. water
½ c. vinegar   6 c. sliced cooked potatoes

Cook bacon till crisp; drain and crumble, reserving ½ c. drippings. Cook onion in reserved drippings till tender. Blend in flour, sugar, salt, celery seed and pepper. Add water and vinegar, cook and stir till thickened and bubbly. Add bacon and potatoes, tossing lightly. Heat thoroughly, about 10 min.

Favorite Macaroni Salad

6 c. macaroni, cooked
4 hard-boiled eggs
2 c. carrots, chopped

2 c. celery, chopped
2 sm. onions, chopped

Dressing:
Salt to taste
2 c. sugar
½ c. vinegar
½ c. water

1 T. margarine
4 eggs
1½ c. Miracle Whip
½ to 1 T. mustard

Mix first 5 ingredients. Stir together first 6 dressing ingredients. Bring to a boil and boil 2 min. Cool. Add Miracle Whip. Stir dressing into macaroni.

Three Bean Salad

1 can yellow beans (string)
1 can red kidney beans
1 c. chopped green peppers
½ c. wine vinegar
    (regular can be used)

1 can green beans
1 c. onions, shredded
1 c. sugar
½ c. white vinegar (regular can be used)

Wash and drain the canned beans; then marinate overnight in rest of mixture. Can also be canned; cold pack 15 min.

Country Potato Salad

4 c. diced and
    cooked potatoes
¼ med. onion, diced

4 hard-boiled eggs, diced
¾ c. diced celery

Mix together:
1 c. salad dressing
    or mayonnaise
1¼ T. vinegar
¾ c. sugar

1 T. mustard (prepared)
1¼ tsp. salt
dab of milk

Blend well and add to above ingredients, mixing just enough to cover.

Weiner Potato Salad

Dressing:

3 c. salad dressing
6 T. mustard
2 c. sugar
4 hot dogs, chopped
3 tsp. salt
1½ c. diced celery or 1 tsp.
    celery seed

12 c. cooked and finely diced
    or shredded potatoes
12 hard-boiled eggs
½ onion, chopped
½ c. milk
¼ c. vinegar

Mix ingredients for dressing and let stand. Prepare second part and add dressing. Keeps well. I use half a batch for a family.

Molded Ham and Potato Salad

2 pkg. unflavored gelatin
2¼ c. milk
1 c. salad dressing
1 T. mustard
2 T. onion
2 tsp. sugar
½ c. chopped ham

½ tsp. salt
¼ tsp. pepper
2½ c. diced cooked potatoes
½ c. shredded carrots
½ c. celery, chopped
⅓ c. pickles, chopped

Sprinkle gelatin over 1 c. milk in saucepan. Place over low heat until gelatin is dissolved. Remove from heat and add remaining ingredients, adding potatoes, ham, carrots, celery and pickles last. Pour into pan; chill. Cut into squares and serve.

Tossed Taco Salad

1 head lettuce
4 tomatoes, chopped
1 lb. ground beef
1 can red kidney
    beans, drained

1 bunch green onions, chopped
1 - 5½ oz. pkg. taco chips
1 - 8 oz. bottle Thousand Island dressing
12 oz. cheese, grated

Mix first six ingredients together. Brown ground beef and drain. Add to salad, toss with dressing. Makes a large salad.

Velveeta Cauliflower Salad

3 c. cauliflower
2 c. peas, cooked
1 c. cubed Velveeta cheese

1½ tsp. seasoning salt
1 c. salad dressing
2 T. cream

Separate cauliflower into flowerets slicing the large ones into bite-size pieces. Add peas. Mix salt, salad dressing and cream; pour over peas, cheese, and cauliflower. Mix and serve.

Bacon Broccoli Salad

2 head broccoli
½ lb. bacon, fried crisp

Red or white onion, chopped fine
1 c. shredded cheese

Dressing:
1 c. real mayonnaise
¼ c. sugar
1 tsp. vinegar

Cut broccoli into bite-size pieces. Add bacon, cheese and onion. Combine dressing ingredients and mix all together just before serving.

Lettuce Cauliflower Salad

1 lg. head lettuce
1 head cauliflower
1 sm. onion
2 c. mayonnaise

¼ c. sugar, optional
⅓ c. parmesan cheese
1 lb. bacon, fried and crumbled

In a large bowl chop up lettuce. Cut up and add cauliflower. Chop onion fine and sprinkle over lettuce and cauliflower. Cover with mayonnaise mixed with sugar. Sprinkle with cheese and bacon. Refrigerate. Toss ½ hr. before serving.

The little acts of kindness–the tender word spoken, the loving touch of the hand, the gentle and winsome tone, the heartsome bit of encouragement–these are the jewels in a woman's crown.

Celery Coleslaw

1 med. head cabbage, grated
½ c. chopped onion
2 c. sugar
2 tsp. salt
2 tsp. mustard seed

1 c. diced celery
½ c. green pepper
½ c. vinegar
1 tsp. celery seed

Mix all together. Can be refrigerated or frozen. To freeze, bring to boil. Let set covered until cooled.

Frozen Coleslaw

1 med. head cabbage, cut
1 lg. carrot, grated

1 green pepper, chopped fine
1 sm. onion, chopped

Add 1 tsp. salt to cabbage and let stand 1 hr. Squeeze juice from cabbage and add carrot, pepper and onion. While cabbage is standing, make a syrup of:

2 c. sugar
½ c. water
1 tsp. mustard seed

1 c. vinegar
1 tsp. celery seed

Boil for 1 min. Let stand until lukewarm, then pour over the cabbage mixture and cool completely. Package and freeze.

Green Tomato Relish

12 lg. green tomatoes
4 med. onions
1 c. vinegar
3 c. sugar
1 qt. salad dressing

12 sm. green peppers
1 c. prepared mustard
4 tsp. salt
½ c. flour

Grind tomatoes, peppers and onions until fine and drain. Pour enough boiling water over top mixture to cover and let stand at least 2 min. Heat water mixture then, add mustard, vinegar, sugar and salt; stir well and boil 15 min. Make a paste of water and add flour and add to above mixture. Cook 10 min. While hot, add salad dressing. Stir well and place in glass jars. Seal while hot. Makes 10 pt.

Cottage Cheese Salad

1 lb. marshmallows   ½ c. milk

Melt the above, then add 1 lg. pkg. cream cheese; stir until melted and cool.

Add:
1 (No. 2) can drained crushed pineapple
1 c. whipped cream

Fold in:
½ c. chopped nuts   1 qt. cottage cheese

Makes 3 qt.

Orange Peach Salad

2 pkg. orange jello   2 c. boiling water
1 - 30 oz. can crushed   2 c. drained sliced peaches
    pineapples   1 egg
1½ c. pineapple juice   ½ c. sugar
1½ c. shredded cheese   1 c. marshmallows
1 c. cream (whipped)

Dissolve jello in water. Drain pineapple. Add water to make 1½ c. liquid. Add ¾ c. liquid to jello. Chill until syrupy. Spread peaches in 9" square pan. Add jello. Chill till firm. Combine sugar, flour, remaining ¾ c. pineapple juice and egg. Cook over low heat, stirring until thick and smooth. Let mixture cool. Fold pineapple, marshmallows, 1 cup of cheese and whipped cream into cooked mixture. Spread over jello. Sprinkle with remaining cheese. Cover, chill overnight.

Leah's Carrot Salad

1 box pineapple jello   2 c. carrots shredded fine
1 can crushed pineapple
1 box orange jello dissolved in 2 c. hot water

Then add juice of pineapples and enough water to make 2 c. Mix all together, chill and serve on lettuce or plain.

Christmas Salad

2 - 3 oz. pkg. or
    ¾ c. lime jello
1 can crushed drained
    pineapples

2 c. boiling water
1½ c. cold water

Mix lime jello with water and add pineapples. Chill overnight.

1 c. pineapple juice
1½ T. or 1½ pkg.
    unflavored gelatin
    dissolved in ¾ c.
    cold water

4 oz. cream cheese
1½ c. whipped cream

Heat pineapple juice to boil and add gelatin and cream cheese. Cool and add whipped cream (sweetened). Put on top of lime mixture. Let cool several hr.

2 - 3 oz. pkg. or
    ¾ c. strawberry jello
2 c. boiling water

2 c. cold water

Put on 2nd mixture after jello is cold and a little jelled. Chill. Serve.

Molded Lime Salad

2 - 3 oz. pkg. lime jello
16 large marshmallows
¼ c. salad dressing
½ pt. whipping cream

2 c. liquid
4 oz. cream cheese
1 - 2 lb. can crushed pineapples

Dissolve marshmallows in hot gelatin. Beat when jelly. Add salad dressing, cream cheese and pineapple to whipped jello. Add whipped cream and mold.

Banana Pickles

Use your largest pickles and peel them. Also take out the seeds and then slice in spears. Pack into jars and pour following mixture in jars to cover pickles.

Bring to a boil the following:

3½ c. water
2½ vinegar
6 c. sugar

2 tsp. salt
2 tsp. celery seed
2 tsp. turmeric

Put in hot water bath for 5 min.

Dilly Sweet Pickles

4 qt. pickles
2 c. water
2 c. vinegar
3 c. sugar

2 T. salt
½ tsp. dill seed
1 - ¼" slice onion

Wash the pickles and cut up into spears or ½" slices. Pack in jars. Then heat the first four ingredients and fill jars with syrup. Put the dill and slice of onion on top of pickles. Put in a hot water bath for 5 min.

Apple Banana Salad

8 apples drained and diced
½ c. chopped celery
juice of 1½ lemons
½ c. nuts

2 bananas, diced
½ c. raisins
¼ c. coconut

Dressing:
1 c. water
¼ tsp. salt
pineapple juice
¼ c. cream

1 tsp. vinegar
1 c. sugar
1 T. cornstarch or clear jell
1 tsp. vanilla

Cook; stir till boiling.

Pistachio Salad

1 - 20 oz. can
    crushed pineapples
1 sm. pkg. pistachio
    pudding

1 c. miniature marshmallows
½ c. milk
19 oz. Cool Whip

Mix together and chill.

Overnight Salad

1 can crushed pineapple
1 lb. grapes or cherries

1 lb. marshmallows

Dressing:
Juice of 1 can pineapple
1 lemon (juice)
1 T. cornstarch

2 oranges (juice)
yolks of 2 eggs
½ c. sugar

Cook this and cool. When cool, fold in:

½ pt. whipping cream (whipped)

Put fruit, marshmallows and grapes in after dressing is cold. Let stand 24 hr. or is also good after standing a few hr.

Tangy Cranberry Salad

1 lb. cranberries
1 qt. water
2 c. sugar
3 c. miniature
    marshmallows

½ tsp. soda
1 tsp. salt
2 - 3 oz. boxes strawberry jello
1 c. diced apples
1 c. chopped nuts

Put cranberries, water and salt on stove. When starting to boil, add soda and cook 10 min. or until all berries have popped. Add sugar, jello and stir till dissolved. Add marshmallows while hot so they can dissolve. Remove from heat and let cool. Add celery, apples and nuts. This needs to be stirred occasionally until it jells as the ingredients tend to float. Put into container to store; the flavor improves each day.

French Dressing for Salads

2 c. white sugar
¾ c. catsup
2 tsp. Worcestershire sauce
1 c. salad dressing

2 c. Wesson Oil
⅓ c. vinegar
½ c. onion (optional)
pinch of salt

Pineapple Cottage Cheese Salad

6 oz. jello (lime or
 your choice)

1 c. hot water

When cooled, add:
1 pt. cottage cheese
1 c. beaten evaporated milk
1 - 8 oz. container Cool Whip

1 or 2 cans crushed pineapples
1 c. chopped walnuts

Pour into mold or dish.

Pepper Relish

6 onions
6 pickles
6 red peppers

6 green tomatoes
6 green peppers

Grind this together, put 1 lg. handful salt in and let stand 2 hr. Drain, add 2 qt. water and boil 15 min. Add 1 pt. prepared mustard, 5 c. white sugar, 1 pt. vinegar, 1 tsp. turmeric. Mix and cook 5 min. longer.

Grandma's Pickles

Step 1: Juice

9 c. sugar
9 c. water
3 c. vinegar
10 qt. pickles

3 T. salt
3 T. kosher dill mix
1 T. turmeric

Mix together then bring to a boil.

Step 2: Wash and slice pickles ½" thick and put in clean jars. Put a thick slice onion on top.

Step 3: Pour juice over pickles. Cook jars for 3 min. in hot water bath.

Bread and Butter Pickles

1 gal. pickles, sliced   ⅓ c. salt
4 lg. onions, sliced

Soak in ice water for 3 hr. then mix together the following:

2 c. vinegar   1½ T. mustard seed
4½ c. white sugar   1 T. celery seed
1½ tsp. turmeric

Bring to a boil, add pickles, and boil 5 min. Put in sterile jars and seal immediately.

Delicious Sweet Pickles

Cover 2 gal. of pickles (5" to 6" long) with boiling water and 4 c. salt. Let set covered for 3 days in a cold place. After three days the pickles will be all shriveled up. This is okay.

Fourth Day: Wash off the salt water and cover with plain boiling water.

Fifth Day: Cover with boiling water again with 1 heaping T. alum.

Sixth Day: Drain alum water and slice your pickles. Mix 9 c. white sugar, 3¾ c. vinegar, and ¾ c. pickling spices to make a syrup. Heat syrup to boiling and pour over your pickles.

Seventh Day: Reheat the same syrup and add 1 more c. sugar. Pour over pickles again.

Eighth Day: Same as the seventh day.

Ninth Day: Same as the seventh day.

Now pack the pickles in jars and put in hot water bath just until water comes to boiling. Turn off burner and let set 5 min.

Mustard Pickles in Sauce

2 gal. cucumbers, sliced
½ c. salt
2 qt. onion, sliced
2 sweet red peppers
2 tsp. turmeric

2 qt. vinegar
5 lb. sugar
4 tsp. mustard
5 T. flour

Slice cucumbers in thin rings, sprinkle with salt, and cover with water. Let stand overnight. Drain. Slice onion and chop peppers. Mix vegetables together; add rest of ingredients. Cook until slightly thickened. Put in sterilized jars. Hot water bath 5 min.

Mrs. Wage Pickles

¼ bushel pickle
18 c. water
4 c. vinegar
2 c. sugar

1 T. salt
1 pkg. Mrs. Wage's Kosher Dill
    Pickle Mix

This recipe makes approximately 15 qt. of pickles. You need approximately ¼ bushel of pickles. Wash the pickles and cut into rings or spears, whichever you prefer. Pack them into clean jars. Mix the above ingredients and heat in a kettle until the sugar is dissolved. Then pour the syrup in the jars over the pickles. Cold pack, process 5 min.

Pickled Beets

Cook red beets with skins until tender. Take off skins and cut into desired size pieces and put in jars.

Brine:
10 c. sugar
10 c. water or red beet juice
18 qt. red beets

2 c. apple cider vinegar
2 tsp. salt

Pour over beets in jars. Hot water bath for 5 min. This amount of brine is for approximately 18 qt. of beets.

Picnic Time

Among my happiest memories are the Sunday family picnics. I wished we could have one every Sunday, all summer long, but it was usually only once or twice a year. We often had it on Ascension Day, in the meadow by the creek, and then again in the fall when it got cooler, and the trees were colorful—this time we picnicked in the woods.

At the May picnic, we had the joyously singing birds, wildflowers, delightfully fragrant breezes, new green grass and budding leaves. At the fall picnic, colorful leaves floated down, and chipmunks and squirrels scampered here and there, and the air was crisp and tangy. In May, we took gallons of fresh meadow tea and garden goodies such as buttercrunch lettuce salad. Little spring onions graced our sandwiches, and sometimes also tiny baby carrots. Thick slices of homemade bread spread with fresh churned sweet butter did wonders for those vegetables.

In the fall, we took jugs of freshly pressed cider, and baked potatoes and baked beans heated over our campfire, and a bowl of sliced tomatoes and a jar of pickles. For dessert it was often ground cherry pie, walnut cookies and grape jam. Dad would tell stories and then we would sing a few songs together. Much as I enjoyed the family gatherings with the cousins along, these family outings were even more special.

Cakes and Icings

Oreo Creme Cake

1 lg. pkg. Oreo
    chocolate cookies
½ c. oleo
2 boxes instant
    vanilla pudding
1 tub of whipped topping
    (Cool Whip

1 c. powdered sugar
1 - 8 oz. pkg. cream
    cheese (room temperature)
3 c. milk
1 tsp. vanilla

Whipped cream may be used if you have cream.

Crush cookies. Put ½ of crumbs in a 9" x 13" pan. Mix cream cheese and oleo. Add powdered sugar. Fold in whipped cream. In a separate bowl mix milk, vanilla pudding. Fold 2 mixtures together, then pour over crumbs. Add remaining crumbs on top. Let set several hr. or overnight. May be served frozen or chilled.

Carrot Raisin Cake

Stir this first, then add eggs and mix in dry ingredients:

2 c. brown sugar   1½ c. oil

Add:
4 eggs
2 tsp. baking powder
3 tsp. soda
1 tsp. salt

½ tsp. cinnamon
½ c. raisins
2 c. flour

Fold in 3 c. shredded carrots last.

Bake.

Frosting:
½ of 8 oz. cream cheese   ½ c. oleo
1 tsp. vanilla   1 lb. powdered sugar

You can add some milk or cream if it is too thick.

Journey Cake

1 c. whole wheat flour
½ tsp. salt
1 egg
¼ c. oil or shortening

1 c. sifted flour
4 tsp. baking powder
1 c. milk

When using sour milk or buttermilk, use 1 tsp. soda and 3 tsp. baking powder. Mix and bake in a greased pan. Serve hot or cold with fruit and milk.

Feather Cake

3 eggs
½ c. butter or shortening
3 c. flour
1 tsp. vanilla

2 c. sugar
1 c. sweet milk
3 tsp. baking powder

Mix all together and bake in 13" x 9" pan 350° for 30 min.

Cream Nut Cake

Beat together:
1 c. sugar
2 eggs

1 c. cream
½ c. nuts

Add:
1¾ c. flour
½ tsp. salt

3 tsp. baking powder
1 tsp. vanilla

Pour in greased pans. Bake at 375° for 30 min.

Indian Summer Cake

2 c. sifted cake flour
½ tsp. salt
½ c. lard
1⅓ c. brown sugar
1½ tsp. vanilla

1½ tsp. baking powder
½ tsp. soda
¾ c. milk
2 eggs unbeaten

Bake in moderate oven.

Crazy Chocolate Cupcakes

3 c. flour
6 T. cocoa
1 tsp. salt
2 tsp. vanilla
2 c. cold water

2 c. sugar
2 tsp. soda
2 T. vinegar
¾ c. salad oil
1 tsp. instant coffee (optional)

Combine all ingredients, but 1 c. cold water, and mix. Add water and mix again. Don't overbeat. Bake at 350° for 35-40 min. Makes 3 doz. cupcakes.

Buttermilk Crumb Cake

Make into crumbs:
4 c. flour
¾ c. oleo

2 c. sugar

Take out 1 c. crumbs. To the rest mix:
4 eggs
1 tsp. vanilla

1½ c. buttermilk or sour cream
1 tsp. soda

Pour batter in pan; spread crumbs on top; bake.

Apple Coconut Cake

4 c. chopped apples
Stir and let this form juice.

2 c. sugar

Then add:
1 c. oil
1 tsp. soda
½ tsp. salt
1 c. coconut

2 eggs, beaten
3 c. flour
2 tsp. vanilla
1 c. chopped nuts

Pour into a 9" x 13" pan.
Bake in 350° oven for 1 hr.

Cocoa Chiffon Cake

Stir until smooth; cool:

¾ c. boiling water   ½ c. cocoa

Step 1:

1¾ c. cake flour   1¾ c. sugar
3 tsp. baking powder   1 tsp. salt
½ c. Wesson oil   7 unbeaten egg yolks

Add to the cooled cocoa mixture:

1 tsp. vanilla   ¼ tsp. red food coloring

Stir with spoon until smooth.

Step 2:

Measure into lg. bowl:

1 c. egg whites   ½ tsp. cream of tartar

Beat until stiff. Gently fold into batter until blended. Pour into ungreased 10" tube pan. Bake at 325-350° for 55-60 min. or until done (cake springs back when lightly touched). Invert cake over funnel or bottle until completely cool. Loosen cake with spatula. Invert on serving plate. Garnish as desired.

Colorful Frosting

1 tsp. Kool-Aid   ½ c. soft margarine
4½ c. powdered sugar   6 T. hot water, approximately

Mix Kool-Aid and sugar. Add sugar and water alternately to margarine. Makes 2½ c. Enough for tops and sides of a 9" x 13" or tops and sides of a 8" x 9" layer cake or 2½ doz. cakes.

Strawberry Shortcake

Sift together:

2 c. flour   6 T. sugar
4 tsp. baking powder   salt

Mix in:

½ c. shortening   ⅔ c. milk
1 lg. egg

(continued on next page)

Spread in a baking dish and cream together:

¼ c. oleo   ¼ c. brown sugar
3 T. flour

Put on first mixture. Serve with fresh strawberries and cream while still warm.

Peach Cake

2 c. sugar   1 c. lard
3 eggs   1 c. applesauce
1 c. mashed peaches

Mix sugar, eggs and lard. Add peaches and applesauce; then add:

1 c. raisins   1 c. nutmeats
3 c. flour   2 tsp. soda
¼ tsp. cloves   ½ tsp. nutmeg
½ tsp. salt   ½ lb. candied cherries

This makes a large cake. Bake 1 hr.

Velvet Crumb Cake

2 c. brown sugar   2 c. flour
½ c. butter   ½ tsp. nutmeg
½ tsp. salt

Mix ingredients together to form fine crumbs. Reserve ½ c. of crumbs for top. Then add the following ingredients to the remainder.

1 c. sour milk   1 egg
1 tsp. soda

Pour into baking pan. Sprinkle the reserved ½ c. crumbs over the batter. Bake at 425° approx. 30 min.

Applesauce Raisin Cake

½ c. butter
2 c. all purpose flour sifted
1 tsp. clove
2 tsp. soda

1 c. sugar
1½ c. canned applesauce
1 tsp. cinnamon
1 c. seedless raisins

Cream butter and sugar together. Beat in flour and applesauce alternately. Stir in clove and cinnamon. Dissolve soda in 1 T. hot water and combine with mixture. Mix in raisins thoroughly. Pour batter into 2 greased 9" layer pans and bake at 325° for 35 min.

Fruit Cocktail Cake

1 can fruit cocktail
2 c. flour
1½ c. sugar

2 eggs
2 tsp. soda
1 tsp. salt

Mix all together at same time. Pour into cake pan. Sprinkle ½ c. brown sugar and ½ c. nuts on top. Bake 40-45 min. in 350° oven.

Then cook together 5 min.:
1 stick butter
½ c. pet milk or cream

¾ c. white sugar

Beat till foamy. Add ½ c. coconut, if you wish, after beating. Pour over hot cake slowly so it will soak into cake. Keeps well and gets more delicious the older it gets.

Apple Pecan Cake

3 eggs (well beaten)
2 c. sugar
3 c. flour
1 tsp. salt
1 c. chopped pecans

1 c. cooking oil
2 tsp. vanilla
1 tsp. baking soda
1 tsp. cinnamon
3 c. sliced apples

Bake in a greased floured 9" x 13" cake pan at 325° for 45 min. While still warm, sprinkle with confectioner's sugar.

Dark Chocolate Cake

4 c. granulated sugar
1½ c. shortening
    or margarine
4 c. boiling water
4 tsp. baking powder

4 eggs
1 c. cocoa
4 tsp. vanilla
5⅓ c. flour
4 tsp. baking soda

Bake at 350° for ½ hr.

Sour Cream Cake

½ c. lard
½ tsp. soda
1 tsp. vanilla
3½ c. flour
1 c. sour cream or milk

1½ c. sugar
½ tsp. baking powder
2 eggs, beaten
½ tsp. salt

Cream lard and sugar; add beaten eggs. Sift dry ingredients. Add dry ingredients and cream to creamed mixture. Blend well. Drop by spoonfuls onto baking sheets. Bake at 350°.

Topping:
¼ c. sugar

1 tsp. cinnamon

Mix above and sprinkle on top before baking.

Carrot Walnut Cake

2 c. sugar
1½ c. cooking oil
½ c. chopped nuts
2 tsp. soda
1 tsp. salt

3 c. raw carrots (shredded)
2¼ c. flour
4 eggs
2 tsp. baking powder
2 tsp. cinnamon

Cream together sugar and cooking oil. Add eggs and beat well. Sift flour, soda, baking powder, salt and cinnamon together. Then add to creamed mixture. Fold in carrots and nuts. Bake in moderate oven.

Butter Pecan Cake

⅔ c. white sugar
3 eggs
3 tsp. baking powder
¾ c. chopped nuts
1 tsp. salt
1 c. milk

1 c. brown sugar
¾ c. lard
1¼ tsp. maple flavoring
2 c. flour
1 tsp. vanilla

Mix and bake at 350°.

Caramel Pecan Cake

1 pkg. German
    chocolate cake mix
14 oz. pkg. caramels
6 oz. chopped pecans

¼ lb. butter or oleo
7 oz. Eagle Brand milk
6 oz. semi-sweet chocolate chips

Mix cake as on package. Bake half the mix in greased and floured 13" x 9" pan at 350° for 15 min. In top of double boiler, melt together butter, caramels and milk. Remove top of double boiler from heat. Cool mixture slightly and pour over baked half of cake. Pour over the remaining cake batter. Sprinkle with pecans and the chocolate chips. Bake for 25 min. at 350°.

Pineapple Nut Cake

1 c. brown sugar
1 - 20 oz. can crushed
    drained pineapples
1 box yellow cake mix

½ c. nuts
½ c. margarine

Mix brown sugar, margarine and nuts and press evenly in bottom of loaf pan. Spoon pineapples over mixture. Mix cake mix according to directions on box. Pour batter over pineapples. Bake at 350° for 30 min. Serve warm with pineapple side up.

Old Fashioned Buttermilk Cake

5 c. flour (pastry)
1 c. lard (not melted)
2 tsp. soda

2 c. brown sugar
1 c. buttermilk

Mix sugar, flour and lard, then take out ½ c. crumbles to sprinkle on top. Then add buttermilk and soda. Dough is thick and sticky. Put in oblong cake pan or 4 pie pans. Bake at 250-300°. Eat warm or cold with milk. Is also good with strawberries or other fruit.

Hired Boy Cake

1 c. sugar
1 c. sour milk
2 c. flour
1 tsp. vanilla

½ c. butter
3 eggs
1 tsp. soda

Dissolve ⅔ c. cocoa and ½ c. sugar in a little hot water. Add this to the sugar, butter, milk and eggs, then add the flour and soda and bake at 350° till done. Good with white fluffy frosting.

Triple Layer Cake

Mix and bake a chocolate cake mix; cool.

Topping #1:
5 T. flour
1 c. Crisco
1 stick oleo

1¼ c. milk
1 c. white sugar

Mix flour and milk together. Cook until thick, stirring constantly. Cool completely. Cream the last 3 ingredients and gradually add to flour mixture. Beat well. Spread over warm cake.

Topping #2:
1 stick oleo
1 tsp. vanilla
2½ T. hot water

1 egg
3 pkg. pre-melted chocolate
3 c. powdered sugar

Mix oleo and combine with the remaining ingredients and beat well. Spread over cake.

Cinnamon Pumpkin Cake

2 c. sifted flour
½ tsp. salt
1½ tsp. cinnamon
1 c. chopped nuts
¼ tsp. ginger
2 c. pumpkin
1 c. vegetable oil
1 - 6 oz. pkg. semi-sweet
    chocolate chips

2 tsp. baking powder
1 tsp. soda
½ tsp. ground cloves
¼ tsp. allspice
2 c. sugar
4 eggs
1½ c. 40% bran flakes

1. Sift together flour, baking powder, soda, salt, spices and sugar. Set aside.
2. In lg. mixing bowl, beat eggs until foamy, add pumpkin, vegetable oil and bran flakes. Mix well. Add sifted dry ingredients, mixing only until combined. Stir in chocolate morsels and nuts. Spread evenly in ungreased tube pan.
3. Bake in moderate oven, 350°F for 1 hr. and 10 min. or until wooden pick inserted near center comes out clean. Cool before removing from pan. Glaze with confectioner's sugar if desired.

Delicious Oatmeal Cake

1¼ c. boiling water
1 c. quick oatmeal
½ c. shortening
1 c. brown sugar
1 c. white sugar
2 eggs

1½ c. flour
1 tsp. nutmeg (if desired)
1 tsp. cinnamon
1 tsp. soda
½ tsp. salt
1 tsp. vanilla

Pour boiling water over oatmeal, let set for 20 min. Cream shortening and sugar well. Add unbeaten eggs, one at a time, beating well after each one. Blend in oatmeal mixture. Sift flour, spices, soda and salt together and fold in. Bake in greased and floured pan for 30-35 min. at 350°. While cake is still hot from oven, mix and pour on the following topping. Then broil for 2 min. or until brown.

Topping:
⅔ c. brown sugar
1 c. nuts
1 c. coconut

6 T. melted butter
¼ c. cream
1 tsp. vanilla

Molasses Cake

1 c. hot water
1 c. molasses
¾ c. cocoa
2 tsp. soda
1 tsp. vanilla

½ c. Crisco
2½ c. flour
2 eggs
½ tsp. salt

Mix all together, pour in pan, bake at 350° for 30 min.

Peanut Butter Cake

½ c. butter
1¼ c. granulated sugar
1½ c. milk
3 eggs
½ tsp. salt

1 c. peanut butter
3 c. flour
1½ tsp. vanilla
1½ tsp. baking powder

Cream together butter, peanut butter, sugar and vanilla. Add eggs one at a time, beating well after each addition. Sift together flour, baking soda and salt. Add alternately with milk to creamed mixture. Bake in 10" or 12" tube pan for 35-40 min. at 350°. Cool pan 10 min. Turn out on serving plate. Especially good with chocolate icing.

Martha's Walnut Cake

Cream together until fluffy:
⅔ c. shortening
1½ c. sugar

2 egg yolks

Sift together:
3 c. flour
¾ tsp. salt

3½ tsp. baking powder

Add to creamed mixture alternately with:
1⅓ c. thin milk (½ water)
¾ c. chopped nuts

2 tsp. vanilla

Fold in 2 egg whites stiffly beaten. Pour into greased and floured pans. Bake.

Fairy Cake

6 egg yolks   7 T. water

Beat 5 min.
Add 1⅓ c. sugar, beat 5 min. more.

1⅓ c. flour, sifted 3 times
1 tsp. salt
1 tsp. vanilla

Add to creamed mixture.
Add 6 egg whites stiffly beaten.
Bake in angel food pan for 1 hr. at 300°.

Eagle Fruit Cake

2½ c. flour   1 tsp. soda
2 eggs slightly beaten   1 c. coarsely chopped nuts
1 - 28 oz. jar mincemeat   2 c. mixed candied fruit
    (I use homemade   1 - 14 oz. can Eagle Brand condensed milk
    3½ c.)

Bake for 20-25 min.

Black Walnut Cake

3 c. sifted flour   1 c. softened shortening
2 c. white sugar   1 c. milk
1 c. chopped black walnuts   2 tsp. baking powder
½ tsp. salt   4 eggs, separated
1 tsp. maple flavoring

Sift together flour, baking powder and salt. Cream butter; gradually beat in
sugar. Add egg yolks one at a time, beating well after each addition. Beat
egg whites until stiff but not dry. Add dry ingredients to creamed mixture
alternately with flavor and milk. Combine lightly after each addition. Fold
in nuts and egg whites. Bake in moderate oven.

Cherry Coffee Cake

2 c. flour
1 egg and milk to make 1 c.
½ c. butter

2 tsp. baking powder
1 c. sugar
1 can cherry pie filling

Topping:
1 c. flour
½ c. butter

1 c. sugar

Mix together flour, sugar and baking powder. Cut in butter as for pie dough. Break into c. and milk to make 1 c. of liquid. Beat. Add to first mixture. Put in pan; then add cherry pie filling. Bake at 375° for 30-35 min. Mix topping and sprinkle over pie filling.

Pistachio Cake

1 box white cake mix
1 box pistachio
    instant pudding mix
1 c. gingerale

1 c. plus 1 T. vegetable oil
3 eggs
½ c. chopped nuts or pecans

Put in 9" x 13" pan. Grease and flour pan. Bake at 350° for 30 min. Cool, add topping when ready to serve.

Topping:
1 Cool Whip or Rich's topping - 2 c.
¾ c. milk
1 pkg. pistachio instant pudding

Mix and pour over cake. Let set a little.

Moist Chocolate Cake

2 c. brown sugar
½ c. cocoa
2 tsp. soda
⅔ c. lard or oil
2 eggs

2½ c. flour
2 tsp. baking powder
1 tsp. salt
2 c. boiling water
2 tsp. vanilla

Sift dry ingredients together, then add oil, eggs, vanilla and 1 c. water. Stir well and add another c. water.

Good Frosting for Cakes

1 c. white sugar
1 c. brown sugar
1 c. sweet or sour cream

Put in some butter and cook till thick enough; stir a lot while cooking it.

Whipped Frosting

2 egg whites unbeaten   1½ c. sugar
5 T. water   1½ tsp. light corn syrup
1 tsp. vanilla

Put egg whites, sugar, water, and syrup in upper part of double boiler. Beat with rotary egg beater until thoroughly mixed. Place over rapidly boiling water. Beat constantly with rotary egg beater 7 min. or until frosting will stand on peaks. Remove from heat. Add vanilla and beat until thick enough to spread.

Strong Chocolate Cake
(A strong chocolate flavor)

2 c. brown sugar   ¼ c. oleo
1 c. buttermilk or sour milk   1 c. cocoa
2 c. flour (level)   vanilla
½ c. hot water   salt
1 tsp. soda

Frost with a good chocolate frosting.

Chocolate Frosting

1 c. sweet or sour cream   1 c. sugar
1 tsp. cocoa

Mix and bring to a boil and add a pinch of soda and let boil until forms a soft ball in cold water. Remove from stove. Add vanilla and 1 tsp. butter. Beat till it holds its form.

Almond Butter Frosting

Cream until butter is softened:
2/3 c. butter   1½ tsp. vanilla
¼ tsp. almond flavor

Add gradually 6 c. powdered sugar.
Stir in 3-6 T. cream to spreading consistency.

Wedding Cake Frosting

2 lb. powdered sugar   1¾ c. Crisco
2/3 c. cold water   pinch of salt
clear vanilla

Beat together till real fluffy, add a speck of blue food coloring to give it a whiter effect.

Cream Cheese Frosting

½ box (½ lb.) powdered   1 - 3 oz. pkg. cream cheese
    sugar   1 tsp. vanilla
½ stick margarine

Mix ingredients. Beat until smooth.

Peanut Butter Frosting

¼ c. margarine   ¼ tsp. salt
¼ c. peanut butter   2½ c. powdered sugar
1 tsp. vanilla   3 T. milk

Cream margarine, peanut butter, vanilla and salt. Add sugar alternately with milk, beating until light and fluffy.

Orange Frosting

2⅔ c. sifted powdered sugar   ¼ c. orange juice
2 T. melted butter   ½ tsp. lemon extract

Mix ingredients. Enough for a 10" angel food or sponge cake.

Lemon Creme Icing

4 T. butter
3 c. powdered sugar
3 T. cold water

⅛ tsp. salt
1 T. lemon juice

Cream butter. Add remaining ingredients and beat till smooth.

Sunshine Cake

3 T. shortening
1 tsp. flavoring extract
½ c. milk
3 egg yolks

¾ c. sugar
1½ c. flour
3 tsp. baking powder

Cream shortening, add sugar, gradually, and yolks of eggs which have been beaten until thick; add flavoring. Sift together flour and baking powder and add alternately a little at a time to first mixture. Bake in greased loaf pan in moderate oven 35-45 min. Use 8" square pan. Cover with white icing.

Butterscotch Nut Cake

⅓ c. shortening
6 T. butter
1¾ c. sugar
2 eggs
1 tsp. vanilla
3 c. cake flour

1¼ tsp. baking powder
½ tsp. soda
1 tsp. salt
1¼ c. buttermilk
½ c. nuts (chopped)
1 c. butterscotch chips

Blend shortening, eggs, butter, sugar and vanilla. Beat until fluffy. Add sifted dry ingredients alternately with buttermilk. Pour into prepared pans. Bake at 350° for 30 min. Add nuts and butterscotch chips last.

Zucchini Cake

4 eggs
1½ c. oil
2 tsp. soda
1 tsp. salt

2 c. sugar
3 c. flour
2 tsp. cinnamon
2 c. grated zucchini

Mix oil, sugar and eggs. Add zucchini then the rest of the ingredients. This cake will turn out best in a loaf pan. Bake at 300° until done.

Summertime Memories

On warm summer days, Mother sometimes made delicious, refreshing lemonade. In those days, there were no packaged drink mixes—she used real lemons. She sliced them thin, then added sugar and mashed them with the potato masher, then added cold water from the well.

In the fall, we took bushels and bushels of apples to the cider press to be made into tangy cider. Mother canned around 150 quarts of grape juice every fall, too. Hot chocolate was our Sunday evening treat, in wintertime. Also, during the spring and summer months, we made several gallons of fresh-brewed balsam or mint tea twice a week.

Taking drinks and water out to the men working in the fields was very much appreciated by them, but was no favorite task of us children, if the sun was hot and if there were prickly, thistly, stubble fields to walk through with our bare feet.

One extra warm day, we got a notion to set our jugs down and go wading in the cool creek before we continued on our way. The boys saw us and tattled to Dad, and that was the end of our bright idea. Those drinks didn't stay cold long, setting in the sun when it was 90° in the shade. Besides, we had been told not to dawdle. Later, when I worked in the fields with the grownups I realized how much a cold drink means to person laboring in the sun. When we were older, we liked to have cookies or bars on hand to send to the field with the drinks, which always brought forth cheers from the boys!

Cookies and Bars

Chocolate Marshmallow Cookies

½ c. cocoa
1 c. sugar
½ c. milk
1¾ c. flour
½ tsp. soda
36 marshmallows

½ c. butter
1 egg
1 tsp. vanilla
½ tsp. salt
½ c. chopped nuts

Sift flour with soda, salt and cocoa. Cream shortening. Add sugar gradually. Add egg and beat well. Add flour mixture and milk alternately beating after each addition. Add nuts. Drop mixture by tsp. Bake in 350° oven. Top with ½ marshmallow. Return and bake 2 min. more.

Frosting:
2 c. powdered sugar
3 T. cocoa

4 T. cream
3 T. butter

Chocolate Cherry Cookies

⅔ c. brown sugar
1 egg
2 T. milk
½ c. oleo
1½ c. flour
½ tsp. salt

¼ c. maraschino cherries (chopped)
2 sq. unsweetened chocolate
½ c. chopped nuts
½ tsp. soda
¼ c. cherry juice

Mix as other cookie dough. Drop by tsp. on greased cookie sheet. When cookies are hot and out of oven place a large marshmallow half cut side down on hot cookie.

Frosting: 1 - 14 oz. can Eagle Brand milk, 6 oz. Nestle Chocolate Chips. Cook in top of double boiler until thick. Add 1 tsp. vanilla. Keep over hot water of double boiler while frosting cookies. Top with a nut.

Grandma's Cookie "Receet"

2 c. sugar
2 tsp. soda in a bit
    of hot water

2 c. sour cream
Enough flour to make a soft dough
½ tsp. cinnamon

Drop by tsp. on cookie sheets and bake till golden brown.

Cowboy Cookies

1 c. shortening
1 tsp. soda
¼ tsp. salt
2 eggs
1 c. brown sugar
1 lg. pkg. chocolate chips

2 c. flour
½ tsp. baking powder
1 c. white sugar
1 tsp. vanilla
2 c. rolled oats
½ c. coconut

Sift dry ingredients. Cream sugar and shortening. Add eggs and beat until fluffy. Blend in dry ingredients, oatmeal, vanilla and chips. Dough will be crumbly. Drop by tsp. onto a greased cookie sheet. Bake at 350° for 15 min.

Applesauce Raisin Cookies

¾ c. soft shortening
1 egg
2¼ c. sifted flour
½ tsp. soda
¾ tsp. cinnamon
1 c. raisins

1 c. brown sugar (packed)
½ c. applesauce
½ c. nuts
¼ tsp. salt
¼ tsp. cloves

Mix together thoroughly shortening, sugar and eggs; stir in applesauce. Sift together dry ingredients and stir in. Add raisins and nuts. Drop by tsp. on greased cookie sheet. Bake at 375° for 10-12 min.

Oatmeal Crispie Cookies

1 c. lard
1 c. brown sugar
2 c. flour
1 tsp. soda
½ tsp. baking powder

1 c. white sugar
3 c. oatmeal
2 eggs
½ tsp. salt
½ tsp. vanilla

Cream shortening, sugar, and eggs. Sift flour, soda, salt and baking powder. Add oatmeal and vanilla. Shape into balls and press down. Bake 350° for 10 min.

Fruitcake Squares

6 T. butter or margarine
1 c. shredded coconut
2 c. cut-up mixed
    candied fruit
1 - 15 oz. can sweetened
    condensed milk

1½ c. graham cracker crumbs
1 c. coarsely chopped walnuts or pecans
1 c. dates
8 oz. cherries cut in half
8 oz. candied green
    and yellow pineapple

Melt butter in 15½" x 10½" x 1" jelly pan. Sprinkle crumbs evenly over butter. Sprinkle on coconut. Put fruit over top of coconut as evenly as possible. Cut dates in sm. pieces and dip in flour so they don't stick together, then put over top of fruit evenly. Sprinkle on nuts. Press mixture lightly with hands to level in pan. Pour sweetened condensed milk evenly over top. Bake at 350° for 25-30 min. Cool completely in pan on rack before cutting in 1½" squares. Remove from pan. Makes 70 cookies.

Chewy Molasses Cookies

2 c. sugar
1 c. butter or oleo

1 c. molasses

Boil these together and cool; then add:
1 tsp. salt   5 eggs
¾ c. boiling water with 1 tsp. soda
1 tsp. cinnamon
2 c. flour to make a thin cake dough

Pour in greased cookie sheets and bake at 300° to 350° oven for 20 min. or until done. Cut in squares and cool. Can be put together with fluffy frosting.

Old-Fashioned Ginger Cookies

1 c. sugar
1 pt. baking molasses
3 tsp. soda
1 tsp. ginger

1 c. butter or oleo
1 c. buttermilk
1 tsp. salt

Mix the above ingredients and then enough flour to stiffen dough, about 5 c. Roll out and bake at 375° for 12 to 15 min.

Cream Cheese Cookies

1 c. butter
1 c. brown sugar
½ tsp. salt
2 c. crushed cornflakes
2 c. oatmeal

1 c. white sugar
2 eggs
1 tsp. soda
1 c. coconut
2 c. flour

Mix and bake.

Filling:
12 oz. chocolate chips
2 T. water

1 c. white sugar
8 oz. cream cheese

Melt filling in double boiler and spread between 2 cookies immediately.

Mountain Drop Cookies

1¾ c. flour
½ c. cocoa
¾ tsp. salt
½ c. milk
1 egg

1 c. sugar
½ tsp. soda
½ c. butter
2 T. water
27 lg. marshmallows

Mix in order given. Bake at 350°. When baked, add marshmallow, cut in half, on top of cookie, while hot. Frost with chocolate frosting.

Chocolate Frosting:
3 c. powdered sugar
1 T. butter

1 T. cocoa
3 T. milk

Put on cookies while warm.

Banana Oatmeal Cookies

1 c. sugar
1 c. mashed bananas
1⅓ c. uncooked rolled oats
1 tsp. salt
½ tsp. nutmeg
⅔ c. nut meats

¾ c. shortening
1 egg
2¼ c. sifted flour
½ tsp. baking powder
¼ tsp. cinnamon

Combine sugar, shortening, egg and banana in a bowl; beat until well-blended. Add rolled oats, sifted dry ingredients and nuts, stirring to make a soft dough. Drop by tsp. onto greased baking sheet about 2½" apart.

Iced Spice Cookies

2 c. brown sugar	1 c. shortening
1 c. milk	3 eggs
2 tsp. baking powder	2 tsp. soda
1 tsp. cinnamon	1 tsp. vanilla
4 c. flour	

Mix in order given. Drop by tsp. on greased cookie sheet. Bake at 375° for 10 min. Ice while warm.

Icing:

½ c. butter	1 c. brown sugar
¼ c. milk	

Boil together 2 min. Add powdered sugar until thick enough to spread.

Maple Buttermilk Cookies

4 eggs	½ tsp. cream of tartar
2 c. brown sugar	5 c. flour
1 c. white sugar	maple flavoring
1 c. butter or lard	1 c. buttermilk
1 T. soda	

I mix the sugar with my hands to prevent lumps. Then add the beaten eggs. Stir well. Add the melted shortening. Put the soda and cream of tartar in buttermilk and stir well. Add half of the flour to mixture, then half of buttermilk. Stir well. Add remaining flour and buttermilk. I put flavor in buttermilk, too. Put on greased cookie sheet. (I have a cookie dropper I use.) Bake at 375° for 15 to 20 min. Makes about 3 doz. cookies.

Unpeeled Apple Cookies

2¼ c. all-purpose flour
½ tsp. baking soda
¼ tsp. salt
1 tsp. vanilla
1½ c. coarsely chopped
    unpeeled red apples

1 tsp. ground cinnamon
1½ c. firmly packed brown sugar
¾ c. real mayonnaise
2 lg. eggs
¼ c. finely chopped celery
1 c. coarsely chopped walnuts

In a med. bowl, stir together the flour, baking soda, salt and cinnamon. In the lg. bowl of an electric mixer at med. speed, beat together the sugar, mayonnaise, eggs and vanilla until smooth. Add flour mixture and at low speed, beat until smooth. Stir in apples, walnuts and celery. Drop by level T. 2" apart on ungreased cookie sheet. Bake in a preheated oven 350° for 10 to 12 min. Remove to a wire rack to cool completely. Store in tight container. Makes about 4 doz. cookies.

Soft Ginger Mounds

4¼ c. flour
1 tsp. ginger
½ tsp. nutmeg
¾ c. sugar
1¼ c. molasses
1 c. hot tap water

2 tsp. soda
¾ tsp. cinnamon
1 c. raisins
¾ c. shortening
1 egg

Cream sugar, shortening, molasses and egg thoroughly. Add blended dry ingredients alternately with hot tap water. Mix well; stir in raisins. Drop by heaping tsp. onto greased baking sheet. Bake at 375° for 8-10 min.

No-Bake Chocolate Cookies

Mix the following:
2 c. sugar
½ c. milk
½ tsp. vanilla

2 T. cocoa (heaping)
½ tsp. salt
½ c. butter

Bring to a rolling boil; remove from heat and add 3 c. instant oatmeal and 1 c. coconut, ½ c. nuts. Mix and drop by tsp. on wax paper. Let cool.

Snickerdoodles

Mix:
1 c. butter   1½ c. sugar
2 eggs

Add:
2¾ c. flour   2 tsp. cream of tartar
1 tsp. soda   ¼ tsp. salt

Roll into balls the size of sm. walnuts. Roll into mixture of 2 T. sugar and 2 tsp. cinnamon. Place 2" apart on ungreased cookie sheet. Bake until lightly brown, but still soft.

Oatmeal Whoopie Pies

2 c. brown sugar   ¾ c. butter or margarine
2 eggs   ½ tsp. salt
1 tsp. cinnamon   1 tsp. baking powder
3 T. boiling water   1 tsp. soda
2½ c. flour   2 c. quick oats

Mix sugar, shortening, eggs, salt, cinnamon, and baking powder. Mix soda with hot water, add flour and oats. Bake at 350° for 10 min.

Fillling:
2 beaten egg whites   1 T. vanilla
2 c. 10x sugar   ¾ c. Crisco

Mix together and put between 2 cookies.

Monster Cookies

3 eggs   1 c. brown sugar
1 c. white sugar   1 tsp. vanilla
2 tsp. soda   ½ c. margarine
1 c. peanut butter   4½ c. oatmeal
1 c. M&Ms

Mix in order given. Drop on greased cookie sheet. Bake at 350° for 12 min.

Pumpkin Gems

1 c. butter
2 tsp. baking powder
2 c. pumpkin
2 tsp. soda

2 c. sugar
2 tsp. cinnamon
4 c. flour

Cream cooked pumpkin, sugar and butter. Add dry ingredients and 1 c. chopped dates, raisins or nuts. Drop on cookie sheet. Bake at 350°. Frost with cream cheese icing.

Poor Man's Cookies

1 c. raisins
1 c. water
1 c. sugar
1 beaten egg
1 tsp. vanilla
½ c. margarine

1 tsp. baking soda
1 tsp. cinnamon
¼ tsp. salt
¼ tsp. nutmeg
2 c. sifted flour

Cook raisins in water 5 min.; add oleo and cool. Then add remaining ingredients. Spread on greased cookie sheet or in an oblong dish 11" x 9". Bake at 350° for 20 min. Cool for 20 min. and cut in squares. These keep well in air-tight container (by themselves).

Crispy Crunch Cookies

2 c. brown sugar
2 eggs
3 c. flour
¾ tsp. baking powder

½ c. shortening
1 tsp. vanilla
1 tsp. soda

Make in balls and press down with fork. Bake.

Peanut Butter Cookies

1 c. peanut butter
    (plain or crunchy)
1 egg (beaten)

1 c. sugar
1 tsp. baking soda

Mix soda in sugar, then add beaten egg and peanut butter. I also add ½ c. flour. Beat well. Make little balls, put on greased cookie sheet. Use an *empty* plastic spool dipped in sugar to flatten them. (Gives a nice design on them.) Bake at 350° for 15-20 min. Makes 3 dozen.

Peanut Butter Chocolate Chip Cookies

1¼ c. Gold Medal all-purpose flour
¾ tsp. baking soda
½ c. firmly packed brown sugar
½ c. sugar
½ tsp. vanilla
¼ tsp. salt

1 - 6 oz. pkg. Nestle Semi-Sweet Real Chocolate Morsels
¾ c. Peter Pan creamy peanut butter
½ c. butter (soft)
½ tsp. baking powder
5 T. milk
1 egg
½ c. chopped peanuts

Preheat oven to 375°F. In sm. bowl, combine flour, soda, baking powder and salt; set aside. In lg. bowl, combine peanut butter, butter, sugar, brown sugar and vanilla. Beat until creamy. Beat in milk and egg. Gradually add flour mixture. Mix well. Stir in chocolate morsels and peanuts. Drop by level T. onto ungreased cookie sheet. Bake 10 to 12 min. Makes about 4 dozen 2¼" cookies.

Apple Walnut Cookies

Cream:
½ c. butter

1 c. brown sugar

Mix:
2 c. sifted flour
½ tsp. salt
½ tsp. nutmeg

1 tsp. baking powder
1 tsp. cinnamon

Stir into creamed mixture. Add:
¾ c. chopped apples
1 c. raisins

1 c. walnuts

Drop by tsp. on greased cookie sheet. Bake at 350° for 14-16 min.

Raisin Pumpkin Cookies

1 c. butter	2 c. flour
1 c. pumpkin	1 tsp. soda
1 tsp. baking powder	½ tsp. salt
1 egg	2½ tsp. cinnamon
1 c. brown sugar	¼ tsp. ginger
1 c. raisins	½ tsp. nutmeg
1 c. chopped nuts (optional)	

Mix together sugar, lard and egg. Add pumpkin and mix well. Sift dry ingredients, add to mixture and beat well. Drop on cookie sheet. Bake at 350°, 10-20 min. When slightly cooled, frost with this icing.

Never Fail Icing:
One stick oleo (1 c.). Melt in saucepan, then add: 1 c. brown sugar and ¼ c. cream or rich milk. Boil together 3 min. Add vanilla and maple flavor to suit your taste. Cool. Add powdered sugar to make a thick, smooth icing. Frost cookies and enjoy!

Butterscotch Oatmeal Cookies

Combine: 1 c. shortening, 1 c. white sugar, 2 eggs, 1 tsp. vanilla, 1 c. brown sugar

Sift: 2 c. flour, ½ tsp. salt, ½ tsp. baking powder and 1 tsp. soda. Mix well, then add 2 c. oatmeal, 1 c. coconut, 1 pkg. butterscotch bits (about 1 c.). Mix altogether. Shape into balls and flatten. Bake at 350° for 15-20 min.

Moist Raisin Cookies

Cook for 10 min.: 1 c. raisins and 1 c. water. Mash raisins and let cool.

Add: 1¾ c. sugar, 1 c. Crisco, 2 eggs (beaten), 1 tsp. vanilla, 1 tsp. lemon flavoring, 1 tsp. baking powder, 1 tsp. soda in a little vinegar, 1 c. flour. You can add ½ c. chopped nuts.

Combine all ingredients. Drop from tsp. and bake 12-15 min. in 375° oven. Will make 3½ dozen cookies. (A moist cookie for lunchboxes.)

Ginger Molasses Cookies

6-8 c. flour
¾ tsp. salt
½ tsp. cinnamon
2 T. ginger
1 c. lard
1 c. boiling water

1 c. sugar
1 egg
2 T. vinegar
4 tsp. soda
2 c. dark baking molasses

Sift 6 c. flour with salt and spices. Cream lard and sugar, add the egg. Beat until light. Add molasses and vinegar, then dry ingredients and soda dissolved in boiling water. If necessary, add more flour to make soft dough. Drop by tsp. on greased cookie sheet. Sprinkle with sugar. Bake 10 min. at 350°.

Pinwheel Cookies

1 c. butter
1 c. brown sugar
3 eggs
1 tsp. soda

1 c. white sugar
4 c. flour
1 tsp. cinnamon
½ tsp. salt

Cream butter and sugar; add eggs, then add dry ingredients. If dough is too soft, chill a while. Roll on floured board ½" thick. Spread with filling and roll in jellyroll fashion. Cool until firm. Slice and bake in hot oven.

Filling:
½ c. dates
½ c. water

½ c. sugar
½ c. nuts

Combine dates, sugar and water. Cook until thick, then add nuts. This may be enough for 2 batches cookies.

Chocolate Sandwich Cookies

2 c. brown sugar
4 c. flour
½ c. butter
1 tsp. soda

¼ c. cocoa
1 tsp. vanilla
2-3 eggs

Roll thin and bake. Spread icing between 2 cookies.

Chocolate Chip Krispies

5 c. flour
1 tsp. salt
4 c. sugar
4 tsp. vanilla
2 - 12 oz. pkg. chocolate
    chips or M&Ms

2 tsp. soda
2 c. butter, softened
4 eggs
8 c. rice krispies

Beat oleo and sugar until smooth. Beat eggs and vanilla. Mix in flour, soda and salt. Stir in cereal and chips. Drop on greased baking sheet. Bake at 350° about 10 min. or until lightly browned.

Mommy's Sugar Cookies

1 c. sugar
1 c. butter
2 eggs
5½ c. flour
1 tsp. cream of tartar

1 c. powdered sugar
1 c. milk
1 tsp. vanilla
2 tsp. baking powder
½ tsp. salt

Cream together sugars and butter. Add eggs and beat well. Beat in milk and vanilla. Sift together flour, baking powder, cream of tartar and salt and add to mixture, mixing thoroughly. Shape into balls and flatten with a glass dipped in sugar or refrigerate and roll out for cut cookies. Bake at 350° for 8-10 min. Frost or decorate if desired.

Farmer Cookies

2 c. brown sugar
3 eggs
2 tsp. soda
3½ c. flour
½ tsp. salt

1 c. shortening
½ c. milk
2 tsp. baking powder
½ tsp. nutmeg
1 tsp. vanilla

Drop on cookie sheet and bake.

Chocolate Whoopie Pies

1 c. butter
2 c. sugar
4 c. flour
1 tsp. salt
1 c. hot water

2 eggs beaten
1 tsp. vanilla
1 c. cocoa
1 c. soy milk
3 tsp. soda

Cream together: shortening, sugar, eggs and vanilla. Sift together: flour, cocoa and salt. Add alternately to cream mixture with sour milk. Add soda to hot water and stir into other mixture. Drop on cookie sheet and bake at 350° for about 7-10 min. (Can make sour milk by adding 2 T. of vinegar to milk.)

Creamy Icing

2 egg whites
(can be omitted)
3 c. powdered sugar
1¼ c. shortening

4 T. flour
1 T. vanilla
4 T. milk

Beat together until fluffy. Spread between flat sides of cookies.

Sand Tarts

1 lb. sugar
1 c. crushed nuts
½ tsp. soda
2 egg yolks
2 egg whites

⅓ c. brown sugar
10 oz. butter
¼ tsp. cinnamon
1 lb. flour

Roll out and cut. Spread with slightly beaten egg white. Sprinkle with brown sugar and nuts and bake at 350°.

Smoky-the-Bear Cookies

1 c. butter	1 c. white sugar
1 c. brown sugar	2 eggs
1 tsp. vanilla	½ c. chocolate chips
1 tsp. soda	½ tsp. baking powder
2 c. flour	2 c. rice krispies
2 c. oatmeal	1 c. coconut
½ tsp. salt	½ c. walnuts

Bake at 375°.

Kris Kringle Animal Cookies

½ c. margarine	5 c. flour
½ c. butter	1½ tsp. cream of tartar
2 c. sugar	1½ tsp. soda
3 eggs	1 tsp. salt
2 tsp. almond extract	2 tsp. vanilla
2 T. milk	

Cream butter, shortening, sugar. Add eggs and beat well. Add sifted dry ingredients alternately with liquid ingredients. Chill. Roll on lightly floured surface. Cut any desired shape. Bake on greased cookie sheet at 400° for 12-15 min. May be decorated when cool.

Pineapple Drop Cookies

1 c. shortening	1 tsp. vanilla
1 tsp. soda	1 c. white sugar
1 c. brown sugar	2 eggs
4 c. flour (more	½ c. nuts if desired
might be needed)	1 c. pineapple (crushed)

Mix and crop by spoonfuls on cookie sheets. Bake in moderate oven.

Brown Sugar Cookies

¾ c. margarine
1 c. brown sugar
1 tsp. cream of tartar
3 tsp. vanilla
1 tsp. soda
2¾ c. all-purpose flour
12 oz. chocolate chips

1 c. white sugar
1 egg
1 c. salad oil
1 tsp. salt
1 c. oatmeal
1 c. rice krispies

Mix until well blended. Drop by spoonful onto cookie sheet. Bake at 325°
till lightly brown.

Pecan Nut Bars

Cream: ½ c. margarine, ½ tsp. salt, 1 tsp. vanilla, ⅓ c. brown sugar, ¼ tsp.
baking powder and 1 c. flour. Press into greased 9" pan. Bake at 375° for
about 12 min. Beat: ¾ c. brown sugar, 2 eggs, ½ c. coconut, ¼ tsp. salt, 1 c.
nuts and 1 tsp. vanilla. Spread evenly over baked layer. Bake 15 min. longer.
Cool. Melt 1 c. chocolate bits over hot water. Stir in ¼ c. light corn syrup
and 1 T. water. Spread on baked mixture and sprinkle with ½ c. nuts. Cool
until firm and cut into bars.

Butterscotch Marshmallow Bars

½ c. butter
1 c. 10x sugar
1 egg

1 c. chocolate or butterscotch chips
2 c. miniature marshmallows

Mix all together in double boiler except marshmallows. Add them when
mixture is slightly cooled. Line a pan with graham cracker crumbs and our
mixture on with the marshmallows on top. Cut in squares when cool.

Walnut Brownies

2 squares (1 oz. each)
    unsweetened
    chocolate
¼ lb. butter
    or margarine
1 c. all-purpose flour

pinch of salt
½ tsp. baking powder
2 eggs
1 c. sugar
½ c. walnuts
½ tsp. vanilla

Melt chocolate and butter together in a 9" x 9" square baking dish. Remove from heat. Stir salt, sugar, eggs, flour, baking powder and vanilla into melted mixture in pan. Mix well. Lightly dredge walnuts in additional flour and mix in batter. Bake at 350° for 30-35 min. Cool, dust with powdered sugar and cut in squares. (Note from Maudie: We made this recipe last evening and it is almost the same as the 4-H brownie recipe. We mixed our batter in a bowl and then poured into a greased and floured pan.)

Amish Lemon Bars

Cream together and press in a 9" x 9" sq. pan: 1 c. flour, ½ c. butter, ¼ c. powdered sugar. Bake for 20 min. at 350°.

Topping: Beat 2 eggs, add 1 c. sugar, 3 T. lemon juice and 2 T. flour. Pour on top of first part and bake 20 min. more at 350° or until top part is set. Sprinkle with powdered sugar after taking out of oven. Cut in squares while warm.

Diagonal Raspberry Bars

2 c. flour
½ c. sugar
1 c. butter (soft)

⅛ tsp. salt
1 egg yolk (beaten)

Jam Mixture:
½ c. jam (raspberry)
¼ c. walnuts (chopped)

½ tsp. vanilla

Combine flour, butter, sugar and salt. Cut together like for pie. Add egg yolk, mix with your hands. Divide into thirds. Shape each into 12" x 1" strip. Make ½" depression with spoon. Spread jam mixture in well. Refrigerate for 30 min. Bake at 350° for 20-25 min. till light brown. Cool, slice diagonally.

Butterscotch Cream Cheese Bars

12 oz. butterscotch morsels
⅓ c. oleo
8 oz. cream cheese (soft)
1 tsp. vanilla

1 c. chopped nuts
2 c. graham cracker crumbs
1 can Eagle Brand milk (14 oz.)
1 egg

Preheat oven to 350°. (Glass pan - 325°.) In med. size pan melt morsels and oleo. Stir in crumbs and nuts. Press ½ of crumb mixture in bottom of greased 9" x 13" pan.

In a lg. bowl, beat cheese until fluffy. Beat in Eagle Brand milk, vanilla and egg. Mix well. Pour on top of crumbs. Top with remaining crumbs. Bake for 25-30 min. or until toothpick comes out clean. Cool at room temperature. Chill before cutting. Refrigerate leftovers.

Pineapple Cream Cheese Bars

½ lb. butter	4 c. flour
¾ tsp. salt	2 pkg. dry yeast
¾ c. water	2 eggs, beaten

Combine flour, salt and oleo. Dissolve yeast in warm water and add eggs. Add to flour mixture and blend well. Knead and let double in size. Divide into 4 balls. Rout out dough.

Cheese Filling:

⅓ c. sugar	1 tsp. vanilla
2 - 8 oz. pkg. cream cheese	1½ T. lemon juice

Combine all ingredients and beat well.

Pineapple Filling:

1 lb. can crushed pineapple	3 T. cornstarch
½ c. sugar	

Cook together until thick. Cool. Spread cheese filling in center of dough. Spread pineapple filling on top of cheese filling. Cut slits on each side of filling and overlap. Put on greased cookie sheet. Let rise 25 min. Bake at 350°. Cool and frost. Sprinkle with chopped nuts.

Frosting:

powdered sugar	vanilla
milk	butter flavor

Fudge Icing

½ stick butter, pinch of salt, ⅓ c. milk, ⅓ c. cocoa, 1 tsp. vanilla. Melt butter, add cocoa, milk, salt, vanilla and enough powdered sugar to make right consistency.

Chocolate Marshmallow Brownies

1 c. butter
⅓ c. cocoa or 2 squares
    unsweetened chocolate
4 eggs (beaten)
1½ c. flour
1 c. nuts, chopped

1⅔ c. sugar
½ tsp. salt
1 tsp. baking powder
1 tsp. vanilla
marshmallows

Melt cocoa and butter together; add all remaining ingredients except miniature marshmallows. Beat well. Bake in large cookie sheet at 350° for 30 min. Remove from oven and cover with miniature marshmallows. Bake until they are nicely puffed up. Frost while still warm.

Peanut Butter Bars

1 c. butter
1 lb. crunchy peanut butter
2½ c. powdered sugar

3 tsp. vanilla
1 lb. graham crackers (crushed)

Mix above ingredients with hands. Roll into lady finger size balls and dip in chocolate.

Pecan Date Bars

2 sticks butter
2 c. sugar
3 eggs
8 oz. pkg. dates (chopped)
⅔ c. maraschino cherries
    (chopped)

2 c. pecans
1 tsp. soda
2 tsp. water
1 tsp. vanilla
3 c. flour
pinch of salt

Mix together and press into greased pan with floured hands. Bake at 250° for 1 hr. and 40 min. Let cool and cut into bars.

Things You Never Regret:
Doing various deed of kindess, offering an apology that saves
a friendship, stopping a scandal that is wrecking a reputation,
taking a time to show consideration to the elderly, and encouraging
a weary fellow-traveler on his way.

Chocolate Crumble Bars

½ c. butter
2 eggs
1 tsp. vanilla
1 c. nuts

¾ c. brown sugar
¾ c. flour
¼ tsp. baking powder
2 T. cocoa (or less)

Mix as you would a cake, spread on bottom of a 9" x 13" pan. Bake 15-20 min. at 350°. Spread 2 c. mini-marshmallows over it. Cool. Melt 1½ c. chocolate chips and ½ c. peanut butter in double boiler. Stir in 1½ c. rice krispies. Spread on top of marshmallows. Chill and cut into bars.

Swedish Nut Bars

1 c. butter
1 c. pecans
1 c. sugar
1 c. graham cracker crumbs

½ c. milk
1 egg, beaten
1 c. coconut

Combine butter, egg, sugar and milk and boil for 1 min., stirring constantly. Remove from heat and add pecans, coconut, and graham cracker crumbs. Mix well. Line an ungreased 9" x 13" pan on the bottom with whole graham crackers. Spread filling evenly over the crackers. Top with whole graham crackers.

Icing:
½ c. melted butter
1 tsp. vanilla

1 T. milk
2 c. 10x sugar

Mix and spread over the nut bars. Cut into squares when cold.

Bachelor Bars

1 c. butter
1 egg
2 c. flour
1 c. chopped nuts

1 c. brown sugar
pinch salt
1 tsp. soda
1 c. coconut

Mix and press into 9" x 13" pan. Bake at 350° for 20-30 min.

Always Cooking

One Sunday afternoon when I was 12 years old, I made up a poem about cooking. I enjoyed cooking for our large family, but must sometimes have felt that it was a never-ending job and that our pantry was always in need of being replenished. Here it is:

Cooking again! Week in, week out,
Three times a day with never a break.
In a matter of hours, we're hungry again,
For we all work hard, especially the men.

There's meat to butcher and donuts to fry,
Applebutter to cook and snitz to dry.
The garden to hoe and vegetables to can,
Bread dough to knead and put into pans.

There's fruit to pick and pies to bake,
Jellies and cobblers and jams to make.
The cows must be milked, for we all like cheese,
And puddins and yogurt and ice cream, please.

There's wheat to be ground into fine flour,
Eggs to be gathered and cleaned, by the hour.
Grape-nuts and granola to be toasted;
Corn, for cornmeal, to be roasted.

Sometimes I wonder what we'd do all day,
If eating wouldn't be an absolute necessity.
No dishes to wash, no meals to make,
No fields to plow, no gardens to rake.

We'd go visit Grandpa's and wear our best clothes,
Sit in the parlour in sweet repose.
We'd talk and visit without a care,
And care not at all that the cupboards are bare.

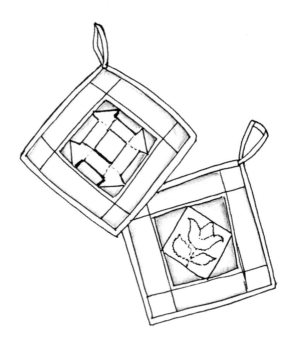

Pies and Tarts

Rhubarb Custard Pie

Make pastry for a two crust 9" pie. Beat slightly: 3 eggs, add 3 T. milk. Mix and stir in 2 c. sugar, ¼ c. flour and ¾ tsp. nutmeg. Mix in 4 c. cut-up pink rhubarb. Pour into pastry-lined pie pan. Dot with: 1 T. butter and cover with lattice top. Bake until nicely browned in 400° oven for 50-60 min. Serve slightly warm. Bake it at 400° for 10 min. and then 350° until done.

Easy Strawberry Pie

Boil for 3 min.

¾ c. sugar
1 T. cornstarch

1 qt. fresh strawberries
3 oz. box strawberry jello
1½ c. water

Stir in one sm. box strawberry jello. Let cool but not set. Put 1 qt. fresh strawberries in baked pie crust. Pour cooled sauce over berries. Top with Cool Whip.

Rachal's Apple Pie

4 c. good pie apples
¾ c. cream
¼ tsp. salt

¼ c. flour
¾ c. white sugar
1 unbaked pie shell

Put apples through second finest Salad Master. Add all dry ingredients and mix. Last add cream and mix. Put in unbaked pie shell. Sprinkle a mixture of ¼ c. brown sugar and 1 tsp. cinnamon on top. Bake 15 min. at 450°, then 350° until baked. Makes 1 pie.

Aunt Anna's Ground Cherry Pie

3 c. ground cherries
1 c. granulated sugar
½ c. brown sugar
⅓ c. flour

⅛ tsp. salt
3 T. lemon juice
½ tsp. cinnamon
⅛ tsp. cloves

Combine ground cherries, sugar, flour, salt and lemon juice; let stand 15 min. Pour into 9" pastry-lined pie pan. Top with crumbs: ½ c. flour, ½ c. brown sugar, ⅓ c. butter or oleo. Bake in hot oven 400° for 10 min. then at 350° for 30 min.

Favorite Pumpkin Pie

3 c. pumpkin
3½ c. hot milk
2 T. flour
8 eggs - beat whites
     till stiff and add last

2 c. brown sugar
½ c. molasses or honey
1 tsp. salt

Mix together and pour in unbaked crusts and sprinkle cinnamon on top. Bake at 400° for 10 min., then 350° for 30-35 min. Makes 4 pies.

Grape Crumb Pie

Unbaked 9" pie shell
1 c. white sugar
2 tsp. lemon juice

4½ c. concord grapes
¼ c. flour
⅛ tsp. salt

Wash grapes, remove skin by pinching at end opposite stem. Reserve skins. Place pulp in saucepan and bring to a boil. Cook a few min. till soft. Put pulp through strainer. While pulp is hot, mix in skins. Stir in sugar, flour, lemon juice and salt. Pour into pie shell.

Sprinkle with oatmeal streusel:
½ c. quick oats
¼ c. flour

½ c. brown sugar
Cut in ¼ c. oleo

Bake 425° for 35-40 min.

Caramel Pie

2 c. brown sugar
½ c. oleo
1 tsp. vanilla
Boil this until the other things are ready.

½ tsp. salt
3½ c. boiling water

3 eggs
1½ c. flour

1 c. white sugar
3 c. milk

Mix this and add to the brown sauce and cook until thick. Pour into baked pie crusts.

Raisin Apple Pie

1 - 9" pie crust prepared in advance, but not baked

4 c. sliced apples	⅓ c. honey
2 T. whole wheat flour	1 T. melted butter
½ tsp. nutmeg	½ tsp. cinnamon
1 c. grated sharp	½ c. raisins
cheddar cheese	

Preheat oven to 350°F. Combine apples, honey, butter, flour, raisins and spices. Put ½ of the apple mixture in bottom of crust. Top with a layer of cheese, then the rest of the apples and the remaining cheese. Bake in preheated oven for 45 min. or until apples are tender.

Old-Fashioned Elderberry Pie

3½ c. stemmed and	⅛ tsp. salt
washed elderberries	1 c. sugar
1 T. vinegar or lemon juice	1 T. butter or margarine
⅓ c. flour	

Pastry for a double crust pie. Spread elderberries in a pastry-lined 9" pie pan. Sprinkle with vinegar or lemon juice. Combine sugar, salt and flour. Sprinkle over berries. Dot with butter or margarine. Adjust top crust and flute edges. Cut vents. Bake in 400° oven for 35-40 min., or until juices show in vents and crust is golden brown.

Rice Krispie Pie

Cream:

2 T. butter	1 c. sugar

Add:

2 beaten eggs	2 T. flour
¼ tsp. salt	1 tsp. vanilla

Stir well; add:

1 c. rice krispies	1 c. white karo

If not enough for 1 pie add a little water.

Peanut Butter Pie

1 baked pie shell
1 c. powdered sugar
½ c. peanut butter
¼ c. cornstarch
⅔ c. sugar
¼ tsp. salt

3 T. butter
2 c. scalded milk
3 egg yolks, beaten
¼ tsp. vanilla
3 egg whites

Combine powdered sugar and peanut butter. Blend until appearance of biscuit mix. Spread ½ of mixture on baked pie shell. Combine cornstarch, sugar and salt; add scalded milk and mix well. Pour this mixture over beaten egg yolks and cook in top of double boiler until mixture thickens. Add butter and vanilla. Pour into prepared pie shell. Beat egg whites until stiff. Spread evenly over pie filling. Sprinkle remaining peanut butter mixture over top. Bake at 325° until brown.

Peach Crumb Pie

2 T. flour
½ c. brown sugar

1 c. sugar (white)

Mix together and put ½ of crumbs in unbaked pie shell. Place a layer of fresh peaches (or canned) on crumbs and top with rest of crumbs; pour cream on top enough to fill a pan and bake.

Double Treat Peach Pie

1 c. sugar
3 T. cornstarch
1 T. butter
1 baked 9" pie shell

6 lg. peaches (fully ripe)
½ c water
whipped cream

Mix together sugar and cornstarch; add water and butter, and bring to a boil. Dice 3 of the peaches and add to syrup; simmer 5 or more min. until thick. Cool. Slice remaining peaches into pie shell and pour mixture over top. Put whipped cream on top. Refrigerate.

Green Tomato Apple Pie

3 c. sliced green tomatoes (do not peel), slice thin
½ tsp. cinnamon
2 c. chopped apples
3 T. flour
⅓ c. white sugar
2 T. butter
⅔ c. brown sugar
1 c. raisins, soaked in hot water and drained
pinch of salt

Put all in a lg. bowl and mix well. Put in a pie crust and bake in 425° oven for 60 min. This is a 2 crust pie.

Fresh Peach Pie

Slice 5 or 6 peaches and soak in a little sugar for a while and then drain. Take the juice and add enough water to make 1 c. Add ¾ c. sugar and bring to a boil. Thicken with 2 T. cornstarch or clear jell. Add a little salt, a chunk of butter. Remove from heat and add 2 T. peach jello and stir till dissolved. Add peaches and put in crust. Chill till set. Top with whipped cream.

Banana Lemon Pie

1½ tsp. unflavored gelatin
3 T. flour
¼ c. sugar
1 c. milk
2 egg whites
3 T. lemon juice
2 beaten egg yolks
½ c. sugar
1 T. oleo
2 sliced bananas

Soften gelatin in lemon juice. Mix next 2 ingredients, stir in milk. Cool over med. heat, stirring constantly until thick. Slowly stir a bit of hot mixture into yolks; return to saucepan; cook a few min., stir often. Mix in oleo and gelatin; cool. Beat egg whites until soft peaks form; slowly add ¼ c. sugar, beating till stiff peaks form; fold into cooled mixture. Pour in a baked pie crust, chill until set.

Coconut Pie

1½ c. sugar
½ c. soft butter
¼ c. flour
½ c. coconut
2 eggs
½ tsp. salt
½ c. milk
½ tsp. vanilla

Sprinkle a little coconut on top. Bake in slow oven at 325°.

Maple Nut Pie

3 eggs beaten
¼ c. soft margarine
    or butter
¼ c. quick oats
½ c. chopped nuts
3 T. flour

¾ c. sugar
1 c. milk
1 tsp. vanilla
¾ c. maple flavored syrup
½ c. coconut

Combine all ingredients except oatmeal, nuts and coconut. Beat well, then add oatmeal, nuts and coconut. Bake in 312° oven 15 min.

Mock Mince Pie

4 slices bread or 1 lg. c.
    (crumbled)
2 c. boiling water

1 c. raisins

Stir and let set until cool.

Add:
3 c. sugar
1 tsp. cloves and
    nutmeg mixed

1 tsp. cinnamon

Mix together, then add to first part and also add:
½ c. vinegar
2 beaten eggs

½ c. butter or oleo

This makes 3 or 4 pies according to the size of the pan. Mixture will be thin but it will thicken as it bakes. This is very delicious.

Peanut Raisin Pie

9" baked pie shell
2½ c. milk
⅔ c. sugar
⅛ tsp. salt
½ c. raisins

4 T. cornstarch
1 T. butter
2 eggs (separated)
⅓ c. smooth peanut butter

Combine all ingredients except egg whites. Cook until thick in double boiler. Pour in pie shell. Topping: 2 egg whites (beaten), ¼ c. sugar, ½ tsp.

vanilla. Put meringue on top of pudding and brown under broiler. (It only takes a few min.)

Apple Butter Pie

3 egg yolks
1½ c. apple butter
1½ T. butter (melted)
1 T. flour
¼ tsp. nutmeg

½ pt. cream
¼ c. sugar
½ tsp. cinnamon
1 T. light corn syrup

Beat egg yolks until thick. Add apple butter and stir in butter, sifted flour and syrup. Blend in cream; add sugar and spices. Pour in pie shell. Bake at 375° for 40-45 min. When pie is cool, top with whipped cream and serve.

Luscious Lemon Pie

2 c. boiling water
½ c. sugar
2 egg yolks
½ tsp. lemon extract

3 T. flour
pinch of salt
2 T. real lemon juice

Mix together flour, sugar and salt. Add a little water to this to make a paste. Then add egg yolks, real lemon and extract. Stir into boiling water and bring to a boil. Add yellow food coloring and 1 tsp. butter. Add a little more water if mixture is too thick. Pour into baked pie crust and top with meringue.

Amish Shoe-fly Pie

1 c. brown sugar
1 tsp. soda (scant)
1 tsp. vanilla
1 c. warm water

1 c. flour
2 T. oleo soft
1 c. molasses
1 egg beaten

Mix well all ingredients. Mixture will divide while baking; pour into unbaked pie shell. Bake at 350° for about 35 min.

Peach Custard Pie

Mix:

1 c. cream   1 c. brown sugar
2 T. cornstarch

Put in an unbaked pie shell lined with peaches. Sprinkle top with cinnamon; add milk till pan is full. Bake in moderate oven till custard is set.

Rhubarb Meringue Pie

2 c. rhubarb   1 tsp. butter
¾ c. cream   2 eggs - separated
1 tsp. vanilla   2 T. flour mixed with 1 c. sugar

Beat egg yolks, sugar, flour, cream and vanilla together. Add rhubarb. Pour mixture in crust and dot with butter. Bake at 375° for 45 min. Cover with meringue made of 3 egg whites beaten stiff and ¼ c. sugar. Bake until meringue is nice and brown.

Impossible Coconut Pie

3½ c. sugar   8 eggs
1 c. flour   ½ c. melted oleo
4 c. milk   3 c. coconut
2 tsp. vanilla   pinch of salt

Pour into greased pie pans and bake at 350° for 45 min. or until golden brown. Makes 3 pies.

Mary's Oatmeal Pie

6 eggs, well beaten   2 c. light brown sugar
2 c. light corn syrup   1 c. butter
2½ c. oatmeal   1 c. coconut
¾ c. milk

Mix all together. Put into unbaked pie shell. Bake 40 min. at 350°. Makes 4 pies.

Criss-Cross Pie

Line a deep pie pan with rich pastry. In a bowl mix the following ingredients:

1 c. apple butter	1 T. cornstarch
½ c. milk	1 egg slightly beaten
¼ tsp. baking powder	sugar to taste

Mix the ingredients well and pour into prepared pie crust. Arrange strips of pastry across the top in criss-cross fashion. Bake in hot oven (450°) for 20 min.

Apple Walnut Pie

1½ c. chopped apples	2 eggs
1½ c. milk	1 tsp. cinnamon
1 stick margarine	½ c. butter
½ c. walnuts	

Mix eggs, sugar, margarine, nuts and cinnamon. Then add apples; mix. Pour in unbaked pie shell. Bake.

Oatmeal Coconut Pie

2 eggs	1 c. sugar
2 oz. margarine	1 c. corn syrup
1 tsp. vanilla	1 c. coconut
1 c. rolled oatmeal	½ tsp. salt

Cream margarine and sugar; add remaining ingredients. Bake in unbaked pie shell for 10 min. at 450° and 30 min. at 350°. Don't make pans too full. Quick to make, delicious to eat.

Laura's Cherry Pie

4 c. cherries	3 T. cornstarch
1¼ c. sugar	cinnamon
¼ c. cherry juice or water	pastry for double crust pie

Cook until thick, stirring constantly. Pour into unbaked pie shell and put top on. Prick to allow steam to escape. Bake at 400° for 30 min. or until done.

Pecan Oatmeal Pie

Beat 3 lg. eggs until light and creamy.

Add:
½ c. granulated sugar	1 c. karo
1 c. pecan nut meats	1 tsp. vanilla
½ c. oatmeal	

Bake 50 min. at 350°.

Quick Strawberry Meringue Pie

Pastry: 1 - 9" baked pie shell. Add 1 tsp. vanilla to crust mixture for special flavor.

Lemon Filling: 1 pkg. lemon pie filling. Follow directions on package. It usually calls for 2 egg yolks. Add one more. This will give you plenty of egg whites for the meringue and a richer filling. 2 c. of strawberries, fresh or frozen sliced. After you have poured the filling in the pie shell, chill for ½ hr. Place sliced strawberries on top of filling.

Meringue: (Preheat oven to 350°.)
3 egg whites	½ tsp. cream of tartar
⅛ tsp. salt	½ c. fine sugar

Beat egg whites, cream of tartar and salt until glossy. Add sugar, continue beating until stiff. Top pie and bake until golden brown.

Rhubarb Raisin Pie

4 eggs	⅔ c. white sugar
½ tsp. salt	2⅔ c. hot milk
1 tsp. vanilla	1 c. rhubarb
½ c. raisins	

Beat above ingredients, then add 1 c. cut rhubarb. Pour into unbaked pie shell. Bake 400° approx. 30 min.

Lemon Meringue Pie

1 c. white sugar
juice of 1 lg. lemon
2 egg yolks
1 tsp. lemon rind

½ tsp. salt
1 T. butter
1½ c. water
½ c. flour

Cook in double boiler. Makes 1 pie.

Meringue for pie:
2 egg whites   3 T. sugar

Put this filling in a baked pie shell.

Sugar Cream Pie

1 c. white sugar
⅔ c. brown sugar
½ c. flour
½ tsp. salt

1 c. boiling water
1 c. thin cream
½ tsp. nutmeg
1 tsp. vanilla

Combine dry ingredients. Add slowly the 1 c. boiling water. Then add cream, vanilla and nutmeg. Bake at 425° for 10 min., reduce heat to 350° and bake until done.

Aunt Sue's Pumpkin Pie

1 c. brown sugar
¼ tsp. allspice
2 T. flour
1 tsp. cinnamon
3 eggs
1 c. cream

¼ tsp. ginger
1¼ c. white sugar
¼ tsp. cloves
pinch of salt
1½ c. pumpkin
4 c. milk

Mix dry ingredients. Add a little milk and egg yolks, mix well. Then add pumpkin, hot milk and cream. Last add stiffly beaten egg whites. Makes 3 sm. pies. Bake at 425° for 10 min. Turn oven back to 400° for 20-25 min. more.

Blueberry Pie

2½ c. blueberries, fresh or
    frozen (a full 2½ c.)
1 c. sugar
⅛ c. flour
9" unbaked 2-crust pie shell

⅛ c. Minute tapioca
⅛ tsp. salt
1 T. lemon juice
2 T. butter

Toss blueberries with all ingredients, except lemon juice and butter. Pour into a 9" pastry. Dribble lemon juice over blueberry mixture and dot with butter. Wet pastry edge with fingertips and cover with top pastry. Sprinkle with sugar. Bake at 350°

Apple Pie Filling to Can

4 c. sugar
2 tsp. salt

8 c. water
8 T. lemon juice

Heat the above ingredients.
Paste made of 2 c. clear jell and 4 c. water. Stir in heated ingredients and boil. Remove from heat and add 4 c. karo, 16 c. fruit of finely cut apples or blueberries or whatever you like. Cold pack this 10 or 15 min.

Chocolate Creme Pie

Make meringue as follows:
2 egg whites
¼ tsp. salt

¼ tsp. cinnamon
½ c. sugar

Spread on baked pie shell and bake.

Cool and put in filling:
2 egg yolks, slightly beaten
½ c. chocolate bits, melted

¼ c. water

Pour half of this mixture on baked meringue.

Combine:
¼ c. sugar
½ tsp. cinnamon

1 c. cream (whipped)

Whip cream. Put ½ of cream on top. Combine other ½ with remaining chocolate mixture. Fill pie.

Pecan Grape Nut Pie

3 eggs beaten
½ c. sugar
1 T. flour
2 T. melted butter
¼ c. grape nuts

¼ tsp. salt
1 c. molasses (white and dark)
1 c. milk
1 c. chopped pecans
¼ c. coconut

Bake at 350° for 45 min.

Clara's Crumb Pie

1 c. brown sugar
1 c. light corn syrup
1 tsp. vanilla

2 T. flour
2 c. hot water

Boil together and pour into 2 unbaked pie shells. Cover with crumbs. Bake in a slow oven.

Crumbs:
2 c. flour
1 tsp. cream of tartar
½ c. butter

1 tsp. soda
1 c. brown sugar

Dutch Apple Pie

3 c. apples (sliced)
½ tsp. cinnamon
2 T. butter

1 c. sugar
1 T. flour
2 T. cream

Mix together and put in unbaked pie shell. Put crumbs on top and bake at 450°.

Crumbs:
½ c. sugar
¾ c. flour

⅓ c. butter

Berry Cheese Pie

1 pkg. graham crackers
1 stick margarine, melted
8 oz. cream cheese
1 can sweetened condensed
    milk

⅓ to ½ c. real lemon
1 tsp. vanilla
1 - 1 lb. 5 oz. can chilled cherry
    or blueberry pie filling

Make a crust with crackers and margarine. Press into a 9" pie pan. Beat cream cheese till fluffy. Add condensed milk. Blend well. Add lemon juice and vanilla; beat till blended. Pour into pie crust as soon as possible as the mixture sets up fast after the lemon juice is added. Pour pie filling onto cream cheese mixture and chill. Makes at least 8 servings. This is very rich, but also very good!

Krispy Chocolate Chip Pie

Beat 2 eggs.

Add:
⅔ c. brown sugar
¼ tsp. salt
1 T. flour
3 T. melted butter
½ c. chopped pecans

½ c. molasses
1 tsp. vanilla
½ c. milk
1 c. rice krispies (heaping)
1 c. chocolate chips

Pour into an unbaked pie shell and bake at 350° for 45 min.

Pie Crust Mix

12 c. flour
4 tsp. salt

4 c. cold lard

Mix well till crumbly. Store in cool place. Use 2 c. mix to 2-3 T. water, and blend well (do not overwork).

Pie Crust

1 c. shortening   ½ c. water
½ tsp. salt (a pinch of salt)

Enough flour to make a dough (2 c. or so) mix together like regular pie dough. The trimmings will not stiffen when rolled out again.

Mommy's Pie Crust

Mix:
½ c. cold water   1 tsp. vinegar
¾ c. lard

Add:
¼ tsp. salt   flour to make a very soft dough

Makes 2 pies with tops or 3 crusts.

Fried Apple Tarts

5 c. flour (all-purpose)   1 tsp. salt
1 tsp. baking powder   1 tsp. sugar
2 eggs (slightly beaten)   1 c. Crisco
1 - 13 oz. can
    evaporated milk

Cut shortening in dry ingredients - mix eggs and milk together, then add to first mixture. Mix with fork just till it holds together - no more. Roll out rather thin. Cut out sm. rounds using a sm. saucer as a pattern. Put a spoonful of your favorite fruit pie filling on one side. Be sure your filling is fairly thick and cold. Fold over and seal edges well. Fry in deep fat until golden brown on both sides. Should make about 36.

Delicious Apple Tart

3 lb. cooking apples   ½ tsp. cinnamon
½ c. non-dairy creamer   1 c. sugar
4 T. flour   2 T. margarine
2 egg yolks   1 T. margarine
½ tsp. lemon peel (grated)   1 pastry shell for 9"

Peel, core and slice apples. Heap in pastry shell. Pour sugar, flour and lemon peel over apples, toss lightly. Dot with margarine and sprinkle cinnamon over all. Bake for 30 min. at 375°. Meanwhile warm non-dairy creamer and margarine together. Cool and stir in the egg yolks. Pour over the apples and bake another 15-20 min. at 350° until puffed and golden brown. Remove from oven and sprinkle with confectioner's sugar. Keep refrigerated but serve at room temperature.

Ground Cherry Tarts

1 c. sugar	2½ to 3 T. Minute tapioca
½ c. water	⅛ tsp. salt
1 T. vinegar	3 c. ground cherries, hulled

Bring sugar, water, vinegar to boil; add tapioca, then ground cherries. Pour into 24 tart shells. Top with crumbs: 4 T. flour, 3 T. sugar, 2 T. butter (rub together).

Vanilla Tarts

1¼ c. sugar	1¼ c. molasses
1 c. cold water	

Divide into 4 crusts (tart shells)

2 c. sugar	1 c. buttermilk
½ c. lard	1 egg
1 tsp. soda	3 c. flour
1 tsp. vanilla	

Bake at 350° for 35 min.

Streusel Pie

Bake 2 pie shells. Take ⅔ c. peanut butter, 1½ c. powdered sugar. Blend together until mealy. Spinkle ⅔ over shells, save ⅓ for top.

Combine:

1 c. white sugar	⅔ c. cornstarch
¼ tsp. salt	4 c. milk
6 egg yolks	

And cook, add ¼ c. butter and 2 tsp. vanilla; let cool. Pour into shells. Beat 6 egg whites until stiff. Beat in ½ tsp. cream of tartar, 1 c. white sugar mixed with 2 tsp. cornstarch. Beat until stiff and pour on pies. Sprinkle peanut butter mixture on top. Put in hot oven till brown. Makes 3 sm. pies.

Raisin Crumb Pie

4 c. raisons
2 pt. water
2 T. clear jell

1 c. brown sugar
1 T. vinegar
salt

Thicken with the clear jell mixed with a little water.

Milking the Cow

When I was between the ages of 11 and 14, my job was to milk the family cow every morning and evening. This was no hardship for me, for I loved being in the barn with its friendly animals, sweet-smelling hay, cooing pigeons and playful kittens. I much preferred barn chores to doing housework, for I was a real tomboy. I think my mother often despaired of ever being able to teach me to be a good cook, seamstress and proper housekeeper.

Milking our old tame Flossie cow was so easy that a 5-year-old could have done it. But one day she slipped on wet concrete and was unable to get up. When Dad said we would have to butcher her, I ran to the woodshed so no one would see me crying. She was turned into juicy hamburgers and dried beef, meatballs and bologna, but for several weeks I was unable to bring myself to eat any. Dad replaced her with a young first-calf heifer who was just the opposite of Flossie. She was nervous and restless, and the strain of never knowing when a flying hoof would send the milk bucket sailing made me nervous, too. Finally I made a bargain with my older brother—if he would milk the kicker for me until she tamed down, I would make him a batch of fudge or taffy whenever he asked for it. He thought that was a wonderful idea, and in just a few days time he had shown that cow who was boss and gotten her into submission. He got his candy, too, which he thought was just great until his next dentist visit. He had 12 cavities, and Mother put a stop to the candy making.

Desserts and Yogurt

Maraschino Lime Dessert

1 - 3 oz. pkg. lime jello
½ pt. sour cream
½ c. chopped nuts

1 c. boiling water
1 c. crushed pineapples with syrup
12 maraschino cherries (halved)

Dissolve jello in boiling water; refrigerate until partially set. Fold in sour cream, fruits and nuts. Chill until firm.

Kool-Aid Dessert

1 lg. pkg. or 4
    scoops Kool Aid
2 qt. water

1 c. sugar
4 heaping T. clear jell

Cook till clear and add:
1 sm. pkg. or ½ c. jello same flavor as Kool Aid. When cool, add fruit. If fruit has juice, use it to mix clear jell. Can be used for Danish Dessert.

Strawberry Fluff

1 - 20 oz. can crushed
    pineapple
1 - 13 oz. can
    evaporated milk

3 oz. pkg. strawberry jello
½ c. sugar
8 oz. cream cheese

Boil crushed pineapple and sugar slowly for 5 min. Add jello (dry) mix until dissolved. Cool till it starts to set. Beat cream cheese and milk until fluffy. Fold in pineapple and jello mixture. Chill until firm. Fills a 9" x 13" pan. Can be served as a salad with lettuce leaf or a dessert. Good on crushed graham crackers.

Orange Marshmallow Delight

1 lg. pkg. orange jello

3¾ c. hot water

Mix and cool till warm and add:
1 pt. orange sherbert
½ pkg. sm. marshmallows

1 med. box Cool Whip

Mix all together; pour in mold and chill till firm.

Delicious Tapioca Pudding

Heat 4 c. milk and 1 c. sugar

Mix:
6 T. Minute tapioca   2 egg yolks
1 c. milk

Add to hot milk; bring to a good boil. Add a pinch of salt, beat the 2 egg whites; slowly fold tapioca into egg whites. Stir a few times while cooling. May add sliced bananas or crushed, drained pineapples or chopped nuts or chocolate chips or plain whipped cream.

Chocolate Pudding

1 c. flour   1 c. dark corn syrup
¼ tsp. salt   2 T. melted butter
2 tsp. baking powder   ½ c. chopped nuts
¼ c. milk   1½ T. cocoa
½ tsp. vanilla

Mix together and put in greased baking pan. Combine ¾ c. brown sugar and 4 T. cocoa. Put on top of first mixture. Then pour 1 c. hot water over both mixtures in pan. Bake.

Pink Lemonade Cloud

1 can Eagle Brand milk   8 oz. Cool Whip
6 oz. pink lemonade

Mix all together and put in a dish.

Substitute for Eagle Brand milk:
1 c., plus 2 T. dry milk   ¾ c. sugar
½ c. warm water

Mix milk and water. Stir sugar to dissolve. Equals 1 can Eagle Brand milk.

Coconut Pudding

4 c. milk, heated, not boiling. Add beaten yolks of 3 eggs, ⅔ c. sugar; bring to a boil. Remove from heat and add 2 c. coarsely crushed soda crackers, 1

c. coconut. Beat whites of eggs stiff, add sugar and vanilla to taste; spread on top while other mixture is hot, then brown in oven. Best when eaten same day pudding is made, when cool.

Rhubarb Betty

Syrup:
1 c. white sugar   1 c. water
2 T. cornstarch

Crunch:
1 c. flour   ¾ c. oatmeal
1 c. brown sugar   1½ c. butter
1 tsp. cinnamon

Add 3 c. rhubarb. Put ½ of crunch in bottom of 9" x 9" pan. Then put rhubarb in. Pour syrup over this. Add rest of crumbs on top. Bake at 350° for 1 hr. This is also good with apples.

Apple Crunch

8 c. apples (sliced)   1½ c. brown sugar
1½ c. flour   1 c. oleo
2 c. oatmeal   1 tsp. salt
cinnamon

Line an oblong cake pan with apple slices. Sprinkle with cinnamon. Mix all the ingredients together and pour over apples. Bake 40 min. at 350° or until done.

Ice Cream Sandwiches

3 eggs   1 c. cream, whipped
½ c. sugar

Separate eggs, beat egg yolks until light. Add sugar; beat well. Beat egg whites until stiff; add vanilla. Fold beaten egg whites and whipped cream in egg mixture. Put graham crackers on bottom of pan and on top. Set out to freeze a couple hr. or overnight. Must have zero weather to freeze. Must set pan outside or in freezer to make them firm.

Crumb Topping

1 c. flour
⅔ c. brown sugar
¼ c. oleo

Mix till crumbly and bake in slow oven. To use as crust under puddings or in layers between puddings or as topping.

Brownie Pudding

2 c. sifted flour
1 tsp. salt
1 c. chopped nuts
1 c. milk
2 tsp. vanilla

4 tsp. baking powder
1 c. white sugar
2 T. cocoa
4 T. melted shortening

Sift flour, baking powder, salt, sugar and cocoa. Add milk, shortening and vanilla. Mix until smooth. Add nuts and pour in a greased casserole.

Syrup:
1 c. brown sugar
1 T. cocoa

1½ c. boiling water

Sprinkle over batter. Pour boiling water over and bake. Serve with milk or whipped cream.

Pineapple Tapioca

1½ c. raw tapioca

Pour into approx. 2 qt. boiling water. Boil 10 min. Cover and set aside till clear.

Add:
1 - 3 oz. box orange jello
1 sm. can crushed pineapples
Add around 1 c. sugar while hot.
Add whipped cream before serving.

Pineapple Delight

1 can Eagle Brand milk
1 can crushed pineapples
1 lg. Cool Whip
cherry pie filling
chopped nuts

Mix and chill.

Peach Cobbler

3 c. sliced fresh peaches
2 T. lemon juice
2 T. butter
4 tsp. baking powder
⅓ c. butter
¾ c. milk

¾ c. sugar
3 T. flour
½ tsp. salt
1 T. sugar
1 egg (well beaten)

Topping: 2 c. flour

1. Put peaches in a greased baking dish.
2. Mix together 1 T. sugar and 3 T. flour. Sprinkle over the peaches. Sprinkle the lemon juice and then dot with 2 T. butter.
3. For topping, sift dry ingredients (2 c. flour, baking powder, salt, sugar) and mix in ⅓ c. butter until mixture is like coarse crumbs. Add egg and milk and mix until just moistened.
4. Drop dough in mounds over the peaches.
5. Bake in a 425° oven for 30 min. Serves 8.

Apple Dream

2 c. apples, chopped
1 tsp. soda
1½ tsp. cinnamon

½ c. nuts
1 c. sugar
1 tsp. vanilla

Mix together apples, sugar and egg. Sift dry ingredients, add to apple mixture. Stir in vanilla and nuts. Pour in ungreased pan. Bake at 350° for 35 min. Sauce: ½ c. white sugar, ½ c. brown sugar, ¼ c. oleo, 2 T. flour, 1 c. water. Cook until thick and pour over pudding as soon as taken from the oven. Serve with whip cream or ice cream.

Vanilla Bread Pudding

8 to 10 slices white bread
2 packs vanilla
    instant pudding
    (4 serving size)
4 c. cold milk
¼ tsp. salt

1 t. vanilla
2 T. brown sugar
¼ tsp. nutmeg
¼ c. chopped nuts
¼ tsp. cinnamon

Trim crusts from bread. Toast the bread and cut into ½" cubes. Arrange half of the bread cubes in a 1½ qt. baking dish. Prepare pudding mix with milk as directed on package for pudding. Add salt, nutmeg, cinnamon and vanilla before beating. Pour ½ the pudding over bread cubes. Add remaining cubes and top with remaining pudding. Combine brown sugar and nuts then sprinkle over pudding. Broil for 2 to 3 min. Chill and serve.

Strawberry Pineapple Delight

1 lg. pkg. strawberry jello
2 cans frozen strawberries
    thawed with juice
½ c. chopped nuts

2 c. boiling water
1 pt. sour cream
1 - 4 oz. can crushed pineapple (drained)

Dissolve jello in boiling water; add strawberries, pineapple and nuts. Pour ½ mixture into 9" x 9" pan or mold. Let set until firm, about 1½ hr. Spread sour cream over jello mixture; pour rest of jello over sour cream. Let set.

Sarah's Apple Crunch

1 c. flour
1 c. brown sugar

¾ c. oatmeal, uncooked
1 tsp. cinnamon

Filling:
1 c. sugar
1 c. water

2 T. cornstarch
1 tsp. vanilla

Mix until crumbly.

Press half of crumbs into a 9" baking dish. Cover with 4 c. diced apples. Cooking filling until clear and thick. Pour over apples. Top with remaining crumbs. Bake in a moderate hot oven, about 350° for 1 hr.

Cinnamon Dumplings

Make a sauce of:
1 T. butter   1½ c. boiling water
⅛ tsp. salt   1 c. brown sugar
½ tsp. cinnamon

Put all in a kettle and let come to a boil while preparing dough.

Dumplings:
1¼ c. flour   1½ tsp. baking powder
¼ c. sugar   ⅛ tsp. salt
1 T. butter   ½ c. milk
½ tsp. vanilla

Sift dry ingredients together; cut in butter; add milk, vanilla and mix. Drop by round spoonfuls in boiling sauce. Boil lightly over low heat for 10 min. without removing cover.

Oreo Cream Cheese Pudding

1½ lb. Oreo cookies (crushed)
2 - 3½ oz. pkg. vanilla instant pudding, mixed according to directions on box.
8 oz. cream cheese, creamed until smooth
12 oz. Cool Whip

Mix pudding, cream chesese, and Cool Whip together. Layer in a dish, starting with cookies and ending with cookies on top.

Ho Ho Pudding

First part: Sift together in bowl: 1 c. flour, ½ c. sugar, 1½ tsp. baking powder and ¼ tsp. salt. Mix with these ingredients: 1 c. seeded raisins, ½ c. milk to make batter. Spread batter in buttered baking dish. Heat together 2 c. water, 2 T. butter and 1 c. brown sugar. Let it boil up once. When sugar is dissolved, pour syrup, hot over batter in pudding dish. Bake in oven 358° for 30 to 40 min. As it bakes, batter raises through syrup and mixes with it to make a delicious sauce. Serve with whip cream.

Cottage Cheese Dessert

1 - 1 lb. box cottage cheese
1 can crushed
    pineapples (sm.)

1 - 6 oz. box orange jello
1 sm. tub Cool Whip

Dissolve jello in 1 c. boiling water. Add pineapple. Next add cottage cheese. Cool, then add Cool Whip.

Peanut Butter Party Dessert

Graham Cracker Crust: 2½ c. fine graham cracker crumbs, 1½ c. sugar and 1½ sticks melted oleo or butter. Mix and press into lg. (3 qt.) dish.

Chill 45 min. in refrigerator.

Filling: Mix together 1 - 8 oz. pkg. Philadelphia Cream Cheese (softened), 1½ c. confectioner's sugar and 1 c. peanut butter

Gradually add: 1 c. milk and 1 - 8 oz. container Cool Whip. Put into dish and freeze.

Topping: Mix ½ c. peanut butter, 1 - 8 oz. container Cool Whip and 1 c. confectioner's sugar. Spread on top.

Mix: ¼ c. peanut butter and ½ c. confectioner's sugar until crumbly. Sprinkle on top. Keep in freezer until ½ hr. before serving. Can be made a day ahead.

Blueberry Cobbler

1 stick oleo
2 eggs
½ tsp. salt
4 T. vinegar
1 tsp. cloves
1½ c. blueberries

2 c. sugar
3 c. flour
2 tsp. soda
1 tsp. cinnamon
½ c. blueberry juice

Cream butter and sugar together; add eggs and beat well till fluff. Sift flour and measure. Sift dry ingredients and add juice and vinegar. Beat thoroughly after each addition. Add berries and stir just enough to blend into dough. Bake at 350° for approximately 40 min.

Simmered Apples

Fill a skillet with peeled and cored apples. Cut in two. Mix well; ½ c. sugar with 1 T. flour. Sprinkle over the apples. Add approximately ½ c. water. Cover and simmer until done. Remove from the heat and add about 2 tsp. butter and 1 tsp. vanilla. Can add a dash of cinnamon. Serve warm or cold.

Strawberry Cloud

1 c. mayonnaise
1 - 3 oz. pkg. cream cheese
24 marshmallows
2 T. strawberry juice
1 c. whipping cream
    (whipped)

1 c. frozen strawberries
    (crushed and drained)
1 c. crushed pineapple

Place marshmallows and strawberry juice in saucepan and heat until marshmallows melt. Beat until smooth and fluffy. (Chill) Mix cream cheese and mayonnaise together; blend in strawberries, pineapple and marshmallow-strawberry mixture. Fold in whipped cream. Pour in glass dish and place in refrigerator until set.

Lemon Crumb Dessert

1 envelope Knox gelatin
1 c. boiling water
3 unbeaten egg whites
1 tsp. vanilla

4 T. cold water
⅔ c. sugar
¼ tsp. salt
10 graham cracker crumbs, fine

Spread gelatin over cold water and let soak 5 min. Add boiling water and sugar. Stir till dissolved. Let cool till it starts to set and is jelly-like. Add egg whites, salt and vanilla. Beat at high speed on mixer till light and resembles thick cream. Turn into a 9" x 12" x 2" dish and chill till set. (12 hr.) Cut into 1" cubes and roll in crumbs. Arrange in dessert glasses and top with Lemon Butter Sauce.

Lemon Butter Sauce:
3 yolks beaten thick and lemon colored- gradually add ⅓ c. sugar; blend well. Blend in ⅓ c. melted butter and 2 T. lemon juice and fold into ½ c. whipped cream.

Raspberry Delight

⅔ c. graham cracker crumbs
1 tsp. cinnamon
¼ c. sugar
1 pkg. unflavored gelatin
1¾ c. milk
¼ tsp. cream of tartar
1 tsp. vanilla
Raspberry Sauce
    (recipe follows)

¼ c. white sugar
⅓ c. butter, melted
¼ c. flour
½ tsp. salt
3 egg whites
½ c. sugar
½ c. heavy cream, whipped

Mix together crumbs, sugar, cinnamon and butter. Press into a 9" sq. pan. Bake at 375° for 4 min.; cool. Combine ¼ c. sugar, flour, gelatin and salt in 2 qt. saucepan. Slowly stir in milk. Bring to a boil, stirring constantly. Boil 1 min. Cool thoroughly. Beat egg whites with cream of tartar until stiff. Gradually beat in ½ c. sugar. Add vanilla. Fold egg whites and whipped cream into cooled mixture. Turn into crust. Chill well. Cut into squares and serve topped with Raspberry Sauce. Makes 9 servings.

Raspberry Sauce:
Drain 2 - 10 oz. pkg. frozen raspberries, thawed. Add water to juice to make ½ c.

Combine with:
¼ c. sugar
1 T. lemon juice

2 T. cornstarch

Cook, stirring until mixture boils 1 min. Add raspberries. Cool.

Cherry Delight

1 - 6 oz. pkg. instant
    vanilla pudding
1 c. whipped topping

2 c. cold milk
1 can cherry pie filing
14 graham crackers (crushed)

Line a 9" sq. dish with graham crackers, filling in to cover bottom. Mix pudding mix and milk. Beat well and allow to stand 5 min. Fold in whipped topping. Pour half of pudding on crackers. Add another layer of graham crackers. Top with remaining pudding and another layer of crackers. Spoon cherry pie fillng on top. Refrigerate at least 3 hr.

Fruit Compote

1 c. fruit - fill with juice
    or water
¾ c. sugar

1 c. flour
1 tsp. soda
2 tsp. vinegar

Mix all together. Put in 8" x 8" pan. Bake at 350° for 45 min. or 1 hr. till done.

Banana Split Dessert

½ c. butter or margarine
    (melted)
2 c. graham cracker crumbs
4 bananas (sliced)
¾ c. butter or margarine
    (soft)
1 - 20 oz. can crushed
    pineapples (well
    drained)

2 eggs
1 tsp. vanilla
2 c. sifted confectioner's
    sugar
1 - 9 oz. Cool Whip
1 jar maraschino cherries (4 oz.)
½ c. chopped nuts

Combine melted butter with cracker crumbs. Pat in bottom of 13" x 9" x 2" pan. Beat eggs approximately 4 min. Add powdered sugar, softened butter and vanilla. Beat 5 min. Spread over crumbs. Chill 30 min. Spread pineapple over cream mix. Arrange bananas next. Cover with Cool Whip. Sprinkle with nuts and garnish with cherries. Refrigerate 6 hr.

Emma's Brown Sugar Pudding

Syrup:
1 c. brown sugar
2 T. butter

2 c. hot water

Dough:
½ c. white sugar
2 tsp. baking powder
½ c. raisins

1 c. flour
½ c. milk

Bring syrup to a boil. Pour syrup into a cake pan. Drop dough mixture into the syrup. Bake. Serve hot with milk.

Tropical Ice Cream

5 lg. ripe bananas (mashed)
4 oranges (cut in sm. chunks and add a little sugar and let set till the rest is mixed)
1 - 20 oz. can crushed pineapples
Approximately 6 c. cream and 6 c. milk
2 c. sugar   ½ tsp. salt
3 T. vanilla
Use 1½ gal. freezer.
Use rock salt and crushed ice.

Pineapple Pecan Delight

1 envelope plain gelatin   ½ c. cold water
½ c. boiling water   ¾ c. sugar
1 c. crushed pineapple   1 pt. whipping cream
chopped pecans   angel food cake (broken in pieces)

Dissolve gelatin in cold water. Stir in boiling water, sugar and pineapple. Chill until jelled. Whip cream. Fold in pineapple mixture. Pour over layers of cake. Sprinkle with nuts. Chill overnight.

Apple Blossom Bake

Mix:
2 beaten eggs   1¼ c. cooking oil
2 c. sugar   1 tsp. vanilla
3 c. grated raw apples   2 tsp. soda
1 tsp. cinnamon   1 tsp. nutmeg, optional
3 c. flour   dash of salt

Topping:
⅓ c. sugar   1 tsp. cinnamon
1 c. chopped nuts, optional

Sprinkle on batter and bake 25-30 min. at 325°. Spread into 12" x 18" jelly roll pan. This dessert may be cut up into squares and topped with whipped cream or eaten with ice cream. When served plain as for cake is a good choice also.

Pumpkin Torte

24 graham crackers,
    crushed
2 eggs, beaten
¾ c. sugar
8 oz. pkg. cream cheese
2 c. pumpkin
3 egg yolks
½ c. sugar
¼ c. sugar
⅓ c. sugar
½ c. butter
½ c. milk
½ tsp. salt
1 T. cinnamon
1 envelope plain gelatin
¼ c. cold water
3 egg whites
whipped cream

Mix graham crackers, ⅓ c. sugar and butter and press into 13" x 9" pan. Mix eggs, ¾ c. sugar and cream cheese and pour over crust. Bake 20 min. at 350°. Cook pumpkin, egg yolks, ½ c. sugar, milk, salt and cinnamon until mixture thickens. Remove from heat and add gelatin dissolved in cold water. Cool. Beat egg whites, ¼ c. sugar and fold in pumpkin mixture. Pour over cooled mixture in crust. Top with whipped cream.

Jello Yogurt

Approx. 5 c. fresh yogurt
1 - 3 oz. jello
½ c. boiling water
½ to ¾ c. crushed fruit
    (same flavor as jello)

Make plain yogurt, but omit unflavored gelatin. Mix jello with boiling water. Stir jello and fruit into warm yogurt. Stir only enough to mix or put into blender on lowest speed, only till mixed. Refrigerate.

Chocolate Marshmallow Pudding

24 lg. marshmallows
    or 240 sm.
½ pkg. chocolate chips,
    ground in nut chopper
½ c. milk
½ tsp. vanilla
1 c. cream, whipped

Heat marshmallows with milk in top of double boiler until melted. Fold in whipped cream, vanilla and ground chocolate chips. Pour into graham cracker crust and freeze. Also good chilled instead of frozen.

Crock Pot Yogurt

1 T. unflavored gelatin
1 qt. milk

1 rounded T. yogurt, room temp.

Sprinkle gelatin over milk. Heat to almost boiling (180°). Cool to a little warmer than lukewarm (110°). Mix in yogurt. Pour into wide-mouth qt. jar. Preheat crock pot. Set jar in and fill crock pot with warm water. Cover. Unplug! Let set till yogurt is thickened, approximately 5 hr. Or, set jar into kettle of warm water and reheat if it cools. A 2-qt. wide-mouth jar may be used for a double recipe. Use an upside-down kettle for a lid on your crock pot, if the jar is too tall and the crock pot lid doesn't fit.
HINT: Always save a little yogurt to make your next yogurt.

Favorite Yogurt

3 c. powdered milk
6 c. warm water
2 pkg. Knox gelatin

1½ c. cold water
¼ c. yogurt (bought or from previous
     batch or 2 pkg. yogurt starter)

STEP 1: Mix milk and warm water in 3-qt. glass bowl.
STEP 2: Soak gelatin in cold water, 5 to 10 min.
STEP 3: Mix ¼ c. of Step 1 with yogurt.
STEP 4: Mix all together.
STEP 5: Put in yogurt maker for 5 hr.

NOTE: I make mine in the oven of my gas stove. You must have a pilot light that burns continuously. Turn oven to warm, then turn off before putting yogurt in. Pilot light supplies needed heat. Takes 5 hr. or more.

Sunshine Surprise

1 - 6 oz. pkg. orange jello
1 #2 can crushed
     pineapple (drained)

1 pt. sm. curd cottage cheese
1 lg. carton Cool Whip

Prepare jello according to pkg. directions. Pineapple juice can be substituted for cold water. Cool. Add cottage cheese; mix well; add pineapple and fold in Cool Whip. Chill until firm.

Cherry Shortcake

2 c. flour
2 eggs
2 c. cherries

¾ c. sugar
2 tsp. soda

Enough juice to make the dough right. A good supper cake!

Amy's Yogurt

8 c. milk - heat to 180°
1 T. unsweetened and unflavored gelatin - dissolve in water
Remove milk from stove and stir in the gelatin; then cool to 108°. Add yogurt (several T. or ½ c.). Put in incubator until jelled (2½-3 hr.); then remove from incubator, beat a little, and put in refrigerator.

Plum Whip

1 envelope plain gelatin
¼ c. brown sugar (packed)
⅛ tsp. salt
2 jars (sm.) stained plums
    with tapioca
    (baby food)

1¼ c. water
¼ tsp. ground ginger
2 T. vanilla
2 egg whites

Sprinkle gelatin over ½ c. water, stir over low heat until gelatin dissolves. Stir in sugar, ginger and salt until dissolved. Remove from heat. Stir in ¾ c. water, plums and vanilla. Chill until consistency of unbeaten egg white. Pour into large bowl, add egg whites (room temperatures). Whip at high at least 8 min. Eight servings - 60 calories each.

Fluffy Minute Tapioca Pudding

Cook together until thickened:
⅓ c. sugar
⅛ tsp. salt
3 T. tapioca

1 egg yolk
2 c. milk

Beat 1 egg white. Slowly add 2 T. sugar while beating egg white rapidly. Add to tapioca mixture. (Crushed pineapples, nuts, and bananas may also be added, or put in layers with graham crackers.)

Fudge Nut Bake

1¼ c. sugar

2 c. flour

4 tsp. baking powder

4 T. shortening

2 T. cocoa

½ tsp. salt

1 c. milk

1 c. chopped nuts, if desired

Mix all together; put in pan 9" x 12".

Mix:

1½ c. sugar

4 T. cocoa

Sprinkle on top of dough; pour 2¾ c. boiling water over it. Bake 45-50 min.

Raisin Date Pudding

¾ c. milk

1 tsp. butter

2 c. flour

1 c. nuts

1 c. sugar

1½ tsp. baking powder

1 c. raisins

1 c. dates

Syrup:

2 c. brown sugar

1 T. butter

2 c. hot water

Mix above ingredients and drop into boiling syrup. Bake 20 min. Serve with whipped cream.

Any Fruit Cobbler

1 T. shortening

1 egg beaten

1 tsp. baking powder

4 c. undrained fruit,
     sweetened to taste

1 c. sugar

1 c. flour

pinch of salt

Put fruit on bottom of pan. Blend other ingredients and put crumbs on top of fruit. Bake at 400° for 20-25 min. in an 8" x 8" pan. Good with ice cream or with milk and sugar.

Apricot Delight

½ lb. apricots
pinch of salt
4 rounded T. tapioca

1 qt. water
1 c. sugar
1 - 6 oz. pkg. orange jello

Cook apricots until tender to mash. Take 1 qt. water, bring to a boil, add sugar and tapioca. Boil till clear. Put in jello; add apricots and mix. Cool; top with whipped cream.

Pineapple Dream

Sift together:
¾ c. flour
1 tsp. salt

1 tsp. baking powder
1 tsp. soda

Beat 2 eggs till fluffy.

Add:
1 c. sugar
1 c. nuts

1 tsp. vanilla
1 c. crushed pineapple

Mix all together. Bake at 350° for 35 min.

Sauce:
Melt ¼ c. butter
Add 1 T. flour, 1 c. brown sugar, ¼ c. water, ¼ c. pineapple juice. Boil 3 min. Add vanilla. Serve with whipped cream if desired.

Vanilla Tapioca Pudding

4 egg whites
1 c. sugar
1 tsp. vanilla
½ tsp. salt

4 egg yolks
8 c. milk
¾ c. tapioca

Boil milk. Add the rest of ingredients except egg whites. Boil 3 min. Then add egg whites.

Pistachio Fruit Salad

1 box pistachio pudding	1 - 6 oz. can crushed pineapple
1 - 6 oz. can fruit	1 bowl Cool Whip
cocktail, drained	2 c. marshmallows

Mix pudding according to directions. Fold in the remaining ingredients. Chill before serving.

Rhubarb Dessert

First layer: Crumble together

½ c. butter	1 c. flour
2 T. sugar	

Press in cake pan 9" x 13". Bake 10 min at 350°.

Second layer:

5 c. rhubarb, cut fine	6 egg yolks
4 T. flour	1 c. cream
2 c. sugar	¼ tsp. salt

Put sugar and cream together, then eggs. Mix and pour on top of baked crust. Bake again at 350° 40-45 min. or until firm.

Third layer:

Beat 6 egg whites; add 12 T. sugar, 2 at a time. Beat well. Add 2 tsp. vanilla and a little salt. Put this on top of baked custard filling and sprinkle with coconut. Bake again until brown.

Pentagon Pudding

2 c. flour	2 sticks oleo
1 c. finely chopped nuts	

Mix together and press into ungreased loaf pan like graham crackers. Bake at 350° until light brown. Cool completely.

Mix:
1 - 8 oz. pkg. cream cheese (room temp.)
1 c. confectioner's sugar
1 bowl whipped cream (or Cool Whip)

Spread on crust. Mix 3 pkg. instant pudding, any flavor, with 4½ c. milk. Spread on top. Top with lg. carton whipped cream and sprinkle with chopped nuts. Chill. Lemon pudding is best.

Raspberry Angel Dessert

1 pkg. raspberry jello	2 c. water
1 c. sugar	2 pt. cream
2 c. crushed pineapple	12 marshmallows
1 angel food cake	

Chill mixture till it starts to thicken; melt marshmallows in jello. Slice cake in a big bowl and arrange in layers. Pour jello mixture over top. Strawberries can be used instead of pineapples. Chill in regfrigerator.

Peach Perfection

1 qt. peaches	1 T. sugar
1 T. flour	½ c. peach juice
1 c. sugar	1 c. flour
2 tsp. baking powder	½ tsp. salt
2 T. oleo	1 egg, beaten

Place peaches in baking dish. Mix 1 T. sugar, 1 T. flour and ½ c. peach juice and pour over peaches. Combine the rest of ingredients and sprinkle over the peach mixture. Bake at 400° till browned. Serve with milk.

Pineapple Nut Dessert

1 c. pineapple juice	¼ c. sugar
2 T. flour	1 egg

Beat egg, add pineapple juice. Mix sugar and flour and blend with juice; heat to boiling. Cool.

Add:

½ c. cheese   ½ c. nut meats
pineapple chunks from which you have drained the juice
1 c. cream, whipped

Steamed Raisin Pudding

4 c. whole wheat flour
1 c. sugar
2 tsp. soda
1 tsp. salt

1 c. raisins
2 c. sweet milk
4 tsp. molasses

Steam 1 hr. Don't lift lid. Good hot with milk.

Lemon Creme Whip

1 c. flour
½ c. chopped nuts

½ c. margarine (melted and cooled)

Mix and pat in baking pan. Bake at 350° for 20 min.

Mix together:
9 oz. cream cheese
1½ c. Cool Whip

½ c. 10X sugar

Mix and spread over cooled crust.

Mix:
2 pkg. lemon instant pudding   3 c. milk (not raw)

Spread over cream cheese mixture. If preferred, top with Cool Whip. Hint: When using instant pudding, heat the milk and cool it before mixing with pudding. It does not have the aftertaste.

Vanilla Wafer Dessert

2 pkg. plain gelatin
1½ c. sugar
2 c. whipping cream
1 lb. vanilla wafers or
        graham crackers, crushed

2 c. milk
4 eggs, separated
¼ c. margarine or butter

Dissolve gelatin in ½ c. cold milk. Scald remaining milk. Combine sugar and beaten egg yolks. Add to scalded milk, stirring constantly until slightly thickened. Add gelatin mixture. Cool. Fold whipped cream and stiffly beaten egg whites into cold gelatin mixture. Mix margarine with crumbs. Cover bottom of pan with half of crumbs. Top with gelatin mixture and then the remaining crumbs. Chill. Cut into sq. and top each with whipped cream and a maraschino cherry.

Cherry Cream Delight

2 c. graham cracker crumbs   ½ c. melted oleo or butter
1 T. powdered sugar

Mix all in a flat 9" x 13" casserole dish; set in a cool place for 15 min.

Filling:
1 box Dream Whip Cream   1 - 8 oz. pkg. cream cheese
    (1¼ c. cream can be   1 tsp. vanilla
    used, whip before   ½ c. powdered sugar
    adding)

Mix together and spread on graham cracker crust; next add cherry filling and chill. Put whipped cream on top. Can also use other fruit filling to suit taste.

Heavenly Dream

Crush:
1 T. sugar   4 c. corn flakes
¼ c. soft butter

Combine first 3 things and save ¼ for on top.

1 pkg. Cool Whip
½ c. sugar
8 oz. cream cheese

Mix and pour over corn flakes

Fluffy Pudding

Separate 1 egg; beat white till foamy. Measure ⅓ c. sugar, gradually add 2 T. to whites, beat to soft peaks. Mix rest of sugar, egg yolk, 3 T. tapioca, ⅛ tsp. salt and 2 c. milk. Bring to full boil in double boiler. Very slowly add to the beaten white, stirring rapidly to blend. Add ¾ tsp. vanilla. Cool 20 min., then beat it well.

Kitchner Pudding

1 c. sugar
3 T. butter
⅔ c. milk
1½ c. flour

1 egg
1 tsp. vanilla
2½ tsp. baking powder

Mix in order given. Beat well. Bake at 350° till done.

Serve with Sauce:
½ c. butter

3 T. flour browned in heavy pan

Add water to desired thickness, stirring to dissolve lumps. Remove from heat and add:
1 c. sugar
1 tsp. vanilla

Sweetheart Pudding

½ c. flour
4 egg yolks
1 qt. milk
4 egg whites
26 graham crackers
¼ c. butter

¾ c. sugar
1 c. milk
2 tsp. vanilla
½ c. sugar
⅔ c. sugar

Combine flour, sugar (¾ c.) and the egg yolks; gradually add 1 c. milk; beat until smooth. Add 1 qt. milk and boil. Add vanilla. Melt butter; add to crushed graham crackers mixture. Line lg. shallow baking pan, pressing firmly. Beat egg whites till it holds soft peaks. Add the ½ c. sugar. Pour cooked mixture in baking pan, cover with meringue. Top with remaining crumbs. Bake in mod. oven at 325-350° for 30 min.

Vanilla Ice Cream

3 pt. whole milk
1 c. sugar

⅔ c. flour

Heat milk. Stir up flour and sugar with a little milk. Add to hot milk and stir till it gets a little thick; do not boil. Beat hard 6 eggs, 1 c. sugar. Add 1 more c. sugar, beat again. Add 3 c. cream, vanilla and enough milk for a 6 qt. freezer. A little karo instead of all sugar makes it good if cream isn't plenty.

Cherry Almond Delight

1½ c. sugar
1 c. oleo
4 eggs
1 tsp. vanilla

3 c. flour
1 tsp. almond extract
1½ tsp. baking powder
1 can cherry pie filling

Mix all ingredients except the pie filling. Spread ¾ of batter on cookie sheet. Spread pie filling on top. Drop remaining batter by tsp. on cherry pie filling. Bake at 350° for 30 min. Drizzle glaze on cherry danish.

Glaze:
1 c. 10X sugar

1-2 T. Milk

Strawberry Ice Cream

Beat together:
2 c. sugar
2 c. heavy cream

5 eggs

2 pkg. (4 serving size) strawberry jello dissolved in 1 c. boiling water. Add enough milk to above mixture to fill a 1 gal. freezer. Any other flavor jello can be used with vanilla added. Use rock salt and crushed ice.

Rice Krispie Ice Cream Topping

3⅓ c. Rice Krispies
1 c. coconut
1 stick margarine

1 c. chopped nuts
1 c. brown sugar

Melt margarine in a bowl; mix in remaining ingredients. Spread in a pan; brown in oven. Serve sprinkled over ice cream.

Ice Cream Bars

2 c. cream
1 c. sugar

6 eggs (separated)

Beat cream, egg yolks, and egg whites separately. Then mix together with 1 c. sugar. Drop mixture onto graham crackers. Top with another layer of graham crackers. Freeze in freezer or set out in very cold weather. Instant pudding may also be used. Makes a large amount.

Butterscotch Ice Cream

4 T. unflavored gelatin
3 c. sugar
10 eggs
2 - 3¾ oz. pkg. instant
    butterscotch
    pudding mix

6 c. milk
¼ tsp. salt
3 qt. light cream and milk
2 T. vanilla

Soften gelatin in 1 c. cold milk; scald 3 c. milk and eggs and stir into gelatin until it dissolves. Add sugar and salt, stirring till dissolved. Add remaining 2 c. milk. Beat cream, pudding mix, vanilla, then gelatin mixture. Mix well. Use rock salt and crushed ice.

Fudge Freeze

½ lb. sweet chocolate
    (Hershey bar)
4 eggs, separated
1 pkg. vanilla wafers

3 tsp. sugar
1 tsp. vanilla
½ c. chopped nuts
1 c. whipped cream

Melt chocolate in double boiler, add sugar and egg yolks, cool at once. Add nuts and vanilla, fold in whipped cream and beaten egg white. Combine chocolate mixture. Line bottom of dish with vanilla wafers, then chocolate, etc. Last, top with whipped cream and nuts.

Dairy Queen Ice Cream

Soak 2 T. or 2 envelopes unflavored gelatin in ½ c. cold water. Heat 4 c. whole milk until hot, but not boiling. Remove from heat. Add gelatin mixture, 2 c. sugar, 2 tsp. vanilla and 1 tsp. salt. Cool. Add 3 c. cream or 1 can evaporated milk. Put in cold place to chill 5-6 hr. before freezing. Fruit may be added if desired. Makes 1 gal.

Yummy Dessert

Bottom Part:
½ c. brown sugar

2 c. flour
1½ c. butter or oleo

Mix together and press firmly into a 10" x 14" pan.

(continued on next page)

Top Part:
3 eggs beaten
¼ tsp. baking powder
1 T. vanilla

2 c. brown sugar
½ tsp. salt
1 c. chopped nuts

Bake until nice and brown on top.

Apple Graham Bake

12 graham crackers
½ c. raisins
2 c. thin cream

8 apples, sliced
1½ c. sugar

Put layers of apples, sugar, raisins and cracker crumbs in baking dish and pour cream over it. Bake in oven.

Apple Raisin Bake

1 qt. apples, sliced
¾ c. sugar
1 c. flour
½ c. raisins

½ c. water
¾ c. brown sugar
5 T. butter

Peel and slice the apples, and pour the water over them. Mix the other ingredients as for pie crust and pour over apples and water. Do not stir together. Bake in a shallow pan 45 min. When cool, cut in squares and serve with ice cream or whipped cream.

Tropical Dream Pudding

3 c. pineapple juice
$\frac{1}{3}$-½ c. heaping cornstarch (mix with water)
Heat juice. Add ½ c. sugar and cornstarch and cook. Beat 2 egg yolks. Add a bit of hot pudding to yolks, then add to rest of pudding. Boil. Add a dab of butter. Cool.
Add 8 oz. whipped topping, orange chunks, bananas, coconut and nuts.

Lemon Cream Cheese Dessert

1st layer:
Mix: 1 c. flour, ¾ c. nuts (chopped), 1 stick oleo. Press into 9" x 13" pan. Bake 20 min. at 350°. Cool completely before adding next layer.

2nd Layer:
Mix: 1 c. powdered sugar, 1 c. Cool Whip, 1 - 8 oz. pkg. cream cheese (whipped).

3rd Layer:
Mix: 2 sm. boxes of lemon instant pudding, 3 c. milk. Beat at low speed until thick - spread on top of 2nd layer. Top with Cool Whip. You may want to sprinkle with chopped nuts.

Here's a poem that was composed by a cousin when she was in the 8th grade:

A Virtuous Woman

A virtuous woman is known by her deeds,
A well-tended garden, free of weeds,
A cup of cold water to a thirsting soul;
A word of encouragement to all, is her goal.

A virtuous woman, a keeper at home;
She scrubs and cooks and cares for her own.
Christ living through her makes her burdens light;
She has a smile on her lips and a song in the night.

A virtuous woman, her spirit is bright,
A rose by the wayside, a beacon of light.
She's far above rubies or jewels that glow,
As she travels the paths of her life here below.

Blessed is the homemaker who delights in building a Christian home. Blessed is she whose patience is renewed continually by the Lord, as fast as it is depleted by the demands of her family. Blessed is she whose housework gives her joy, and working for her loved ones is her delight. Blessed is she in whose tongue is the law of kindness, and through whom God can reveal loving wisdom. Her price is far above rubies, and her loved ones shall call her blessed.   –Author unknown

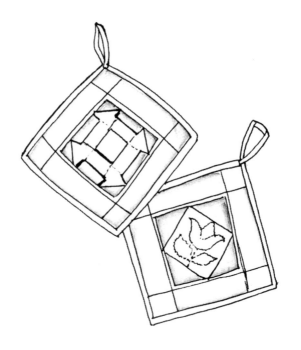

Candy and Snacks

Popped Corn Crunch

½ c. King syrup
½ c. Brer Rabbit molasses
1 c. sugar
1 c. peanuts
5 qt. popped corn

1 tsp. vinegar
2 T. water
1 T. butter
¼ tsp. soda

Mix molasses, butter, sugar, vinegar and water. Cook until it forms a hard ball in cold water (255°). Stir frequently during last part of cooking to prevent scorching. Remove from heat and add soda. Stir lightly, pour over popped corn in a buttered flat pan. When cool, break up in sm. pieces.

Million Dollar Fudge

Put the following 4 ingredients in a lg. bowl and set aside: 4 oz. chocolate chips, 12 oz. German sweet chocolate (cut up), 1⅓ c. marshmallow cream, ¾ c. nut meats. Put the next ingredients into a saucepan and bring to a boil for 6 min.: 1⅓ c. granulated sugar, pinch of salt, ⅔ T. margarine, 4⅓ oz. evaporated milk. Stir hot mixture into lg. bowl mixture and stir until well blended. Pour into greased pan. Cut into squares and store in refrigerator. Note: Hershey's coating chocolate can be substituted for the chocolate chips and German sweet chocolate.

Candy Corn

1 c. sorghum molasses
pinch of salt
alum (size of a bullet)

1 c. sugar (or less)
½ c. butter
4 qt. popped corn

Cook in skillet until thick enough. Add ½ tsp. soda. Pour over popcorn and mix.

Cracker Jack

2 c. brown sugar
½ pt. water

4 T. molasses
Butter, size of an egg

Put in butter pan with 1 tsp. cream of tartar. Boil until spins a thread, remove from heat and stir in ½ tsp. soda. Then pour syrup over popcorn. Stir and dry in oven.

Pecan Creams

9 to 12 oz. sm. pecan halves
2 c. sugar
½ tsp. salt
1 tsp. vanilla

2 c. light cream
1 c. light or dark corn syrup
⅓ c. butter or oleo
1 pkg. milk chocolate

In a large heavy saucepan, heat cream to lukewarm. Pour out 1 c. and reserve. To remaining cream in saucepan, add sugar, corn syrup and salt. Cook and stir constantly over moderate heat until mixture boils. Very slowly add - stir in reserved c. cream to mixture so does not stop boiling, cook and stir 5 min. more, then stir in butter, ½ tsp. at a time. Turn heat low. Boil gently and stir constantly until temperature reaches 248° on a candy thermometer. Remove from heat and stir in nuts. Pour on buttered cookie sheet, let cool about 10 min. Melt chocolate, cut candy and roll in soft chocolate.

Peanut Fudge

½ c. water
1 - 12 oz. jar crunchy
    peanut butter
1 tsp. vanilla

1 lb. confectioner's sugar
1 tsp. butter
1 - 7 oz. jar marshmallow whip

Boil water and powdered sugar for 2 min. Add remaining ingredients. Mix well and pour into a buttered pan. When set, cut in sm. pieces.

Texas Jack

1 c. cream
1 c. sugar

1 c. white syrup

Cook to softball stage and pour over the following:

5 c. cornflakes
1 c. chopped nuts

2 c. Rice Krispies
1 c. coconut

Mix all together and flatten out in pans; cut in squares.

Peanut Butter Krispy Candy

½ c. sugar and ½ c. light corn syrup - cook stirring constantly until mixture boils. Remove from heat and add ½ c. peanut butter, ½ tsp. vanilla. Pour at once over 3 c. Rice Krispies. Pat evenly into buttered 8" square pan. Cool and cut in squares.

Party Mix

1 box Rice Chex
¾ box Corn Chex
½ box Cheerios
2 sticks oleo
1 tsp. salt

1 box thin pretzels
1 pkg. cheese curls
2 T. Worcestershire sauce
1 tsp. celery salt

Melt oleo, add salt and sauce. (Nuts may be added.) Mix well. Pour over cereal mixture and mix. Put in pans and heat in oven at 250° for 1½ hr. stirring every 15 min.

Chex Mix

Mix together:
½ box Cheerios
½ box Rice Chex
peanuts or cashews

½ box Corn Chex
2 boxes pretzels

Stir in ½ lb. melted margarine and 2 T. Worcestershire sauce. Bake in 350° oven for 30 min., stirring often.

Then mix:
2 tsp. celery salt
1 tsp. sour cream and onion

2 tsp. seasoned salt

Sprinkle over party mix and return to oven for 15 min. or more.

Butterscotch Squares

Melt: 1 - 6 oz. pkg. (1 c.) Nestle's butterscotch morsels with ½ c. peanut butter in a heavy saucepan, over low heat. Stir until blended. Stir in 4 c. Rice Krispies cereal. Press half of mixture into buttered 8" square pan. Chill. Set remainder aside. Stir over hot water (double boiler): one 6 oz. pkg. (1 c.) chocolate chips, ½ c. sifted confectioner's sugar, 2 T. butter, 1 T. water, until chocolate melts. Spread over chilled mixture. Top with reserved mixture. Chill. Cut in 1½" squares. Yields: 25 squares.

Crunchy Nut Chews

1 c. flour	2 T. brown sugar
½ c. butter	½ tsp. vanilla

Mix well, pat firmly in 9" x 9" pan and bake 15 min. Remove, pour on the following:

2 eggs, beaten	1½ c. brown sugar
¼ c. coconut	2 T. flour
½ tsp. vanilla	1 c. nuts

Bake 30 min. at 350°.

Pecan Turtles

1 c. pecan halves	1 - 14 oz. bag of Kraft caramels
3 - 1.45 oz. milk chocolate candy bars	1 T. milk

Cut candy bars into twelfths. Arrange clusters of five pecans on greased wax paper. Melt caramels with milk in heavy saucepan over low heat, stir frequently until smooth. Let stand at room temperature 3 to 5 min. or until thickened. Drop heaping teaspoonfuls of caramel mixture onto each pecan arrangement. Top with chocolate. Spread chocolate evenly over caramel. Cool. Store in refrigerator. Yields about 2 doz.

Butterscotch Trix

Melt 1 stick oleo, then add 40 to 45 large marshmallows. After they have melted, add 4 c. Rice Krispies and 3 c. Trix and a handful of butterscotch chips. Mix and press into 9" x 13" buttered dish. Cut in squares and serve.

Chocolate Eggs

1 lb. butter or oleo	1 can Eagle Brand milk
dash of salt	6 to 8 lb. of powdered sugar

Add enough powdered sugar to handle easy. Work with hands. Divide in portions and add different flavors maple, cherries, or nuts. Make in egg shape and cover with melted chocolate. Delicious!

Taffy Apples

1 - 14 oz. can sweetened
    condensed milk
    (Borden's)

1½ c. white Karo syrup
1 c. white sugar

Cook to (firm) softball stage, stirring constantly. Add 1 tsp. vanilla. Cool slightly and dip the apples.

Coconut Flake Drops

1 c. sugar
½ c. cream
1 c. coconut

1 c. light corn syrup
4 c. cornflakes
1 c. chopped nut meats

Cook sugar, syrup and cream to a softball stage. Then stir in the remaining ingredients. Mix well and drop by teaspoonfuls on waxed paper. Makes 4 doz.

Mint Patties

1 box powdered sugar
2 tsp. cream
1 T. soft butter

1 egg white (unbeaten)
1 tsp. vanilla
3 drops peppermint oil

Mix together real good and shape in patties. Dip in chocolate.

Fruity Squares

1 pkg. (3 oz.) fruit
    flavored jello
⅓ c. light corn syrup

2 T. soft butter
4 c. Cheerios

Butter a 9" square pan. In a large saucepan blend gelatin (dry mix), corn syrup and butter. Heat to boiling over med. heat, stirring constantly. Remove from heat, stir in Cheerios until thoroughly coated. Spread mixture in pan. When set about 30 min., cut in squares. Makes about 3 doz.

Peanut Cheese Tidbits

Melt together: ½ c. butter, 1½ c. vegetable oil, 2 T. Worcestershire sauce

Pour over and mix: 7 oz. Cheerios, 7 oz. wheat or corn Chex, 7 oz. rice Chex. Salt according to taste. Put in oven (in a large roaster) at 250° for 1hr., stirring every 15 min. Then add 7 oz. thin pretzels. Roast 15 min. Add 1½-2 lb. peanuts and one box cheese tidbits and roast 15 min. After cooling, store in tightly covered container. A delicious snack!

Hot Cheese Squares

Beat well 5 eggs, add ¼ c. flour, dash of salt, ½ tsp. baking powder, 2 c. shredded Jack cheese, 1 c. cottage cheese (or ricotta cheese), 4 oz. can chopped chili peppers and 1 c. melted butter. Butter a 9" square pan. Pour ingredients in baking dish and bake 15 min. at 400° or 350° for 30 min. or until lightly browned. Cut in 1" squares and use as a finger food. Eat while warm.

Butter Nut Fudge

2 c. sugar
1 c. buttermilk
2 T. white syrup

1 tsp. soda
¼ lb. butter

Mix buttermilk, sugar and syrup in pan, add butter. Cook until it comes to a full boil, then add soda. Cook to softball stage. Cool, then add 1 tsp. vanilla and ½ c. nuts and beat. (Cook in large pan because it boils up when soda is added.)

Marshmallow Popcorn Balls

1 c. brown sugar packed
1 stick margarine

8 c. miniature marshmallows
8 qt. popped corn

Melt brown sugar, marshmallows and margarine in saucepan of top of stove. Pour over popcorn. Butter hands and mix to form the size balls you prefer. Place on waxed paper and cook till they aren't sticky anymore. Store in airtight containers.

Crispy Ice Cream Treats

½ c. corn syrup, ½ c. peanut butter - mix well, then add 4 c. Rice Krispies, stir until well coated. Wet hands with cold water then press mixture in a 13" x 9" x 2" cake pan. Put in freezer or coldest part of refrigerator for 15 min. Cut in squares. Put ice cream between two squares. Delicious with vanilla or chocolate ice cream on a hot day!

Pecan Cheese Rolls

3 oz. cream cheese   ¼ lb. butter or margarine
1 c. flour

Mix together and form 24 balls, then press into muffin tins.

2 eggs, slightly beaten   1½ c. brown sugar
2 T. melted butter   ½ tsp. vanilla
pinch of salt

Put ½ tsp. chopped pecans or other nuts on cream cheese mixture and pour in second mixture. Bake at 350° for 30 min.

Toasted Caramel Corn

15 c. popped popcorn   ¼ c. light corn syrup
½ tsp. salt   ½ c. oleo
1 c. brown sugar   ½ tsp. soda

Combine oleo, brown sugar, corn syrup and salt. When it starts to bubble around the edges, time it for 5 min. Take off of heat and add soda. Stir till foamy, then pour on popcorn. Stir well. Put on cookie sheets and bake until brown, stirring often.

Funnel Cakes

2 eggs, beaten   2 T. sugar
1 c. milk   ¼ tsp. salt
2 c. flour   ¼ tsp. baking powder

Mix together. Batter should be thin to run through funnel. Drop in unbroken stream into hot fat. Turn. Serve with powdered sugar.

Chocolate Crackers

We buy semi-sweet chocolate or almond bark and coat pretzel rods or Ritz crackers. The crackers could be filled with marshmallow creme or peanut butter.

Holiday Cherry Squares

1½ c. Kellogg's Corn
    Flake crumbs
3 T. sugar
½ c. softened butter
    or margarine

2 c. miniature marshmallows
¾ c. chopped maraschino cherries
    (one 10 oz. jar)
1 c. Eagle Brand sweetened milk
1⅓ c. flaked coconut
1 c. chopped nuts

In a 13" x 9" x 2" pan, combine crumbs, butter and sugar. Press down firmly with back of spoon. Sprinkle coconut, marshmallows and cherries evenly over crust. Pour milk evenly over top. Sprinkle with nuts, pressing them lightly into mixture. Bake 25 min. at 350° or until lightly brown. Refrigerate before cutting into squares.

Fudge Snacks

1 c. butter
2 c. sugar
4 eggs, separated
½ c. cocoa

1 c. flour
1 c. nuts
¼ tsp. salt
1 tsp. vanilla

Cream butter, sugar and vanilla. Add egg yolks and beat. Add dry ingredients. Add nuts and fold in beaten egg whites. Bake at 350° for 30 min. These freeze well.

Glazed Walnuts

1 egg white
2 T. cinnamon

½ c. white sugar
2 c. walnut meats (big pieces)

Beat egg whites until frothy - add sugar, cinnamon and nuts. Mix well. Put in flat pan in slow oven (200°), stirring frequently. Bake until dry and crusty. (Will appear dull.)

Cherry Nut Chews

1 c. sifted flour	½ tsp. baking powder
½ c. butter	¼ tsp. salt
3 T. confectioner's sugar	1 tsp. vanilla
2 eggs, beaten slightly	¾ c. chopped nuts
1 c. sugar	½ c. coconut
¼ c. flour	½ c. quartered maraschino cherries

Mix butter, flour and sugar until smooth. Spread thin with fingers in an 8" or 9" square pan. Bake at 350° about 25 min. Stir rest of ingredients into eggs. Spread over top of baked pastry. Bake at 350° for 25 min. Cool and cut into bars.

Popcorn Crunch

Cook together until it forms a softball in cold water: 1 c. brown sugar, 1 c. white Karo and 1 c. sweet cream. Then add knife pint of soda and pinch of salt. Pour over dishpan of popped corn stirrings as you pour. Bake at 350° till it rattles when you stir. Stir a few times in the oven so it won't burn. You may want to put it on cookie sheet or flat pan.

Jello Popsicles

1 pkg. (3 oz.) jello	2 c. cold water
2 c. boiling water	1 pkg. Kool-Aid
1 c. sugar	

Add boiling water to jello, sugar and Kool-Aid. Then add cold water. Pour into containers and freeze.

Apple Snacks

Sift together: 2 c. flour, 2 tsp. baking powder and 1 tsp. salt. Work this into 2 T. lard, 2 T. butter. Add milk to make soft dough. Roll and spread with melted butter, brown sugar, chopped apples and sprinkle cinnamon on top. Roll this up like a jelly roll. Cut slices ¼" thick. Place in baking dish. Make a sauce of 1 c. sugar mixed with 1 T. flour, 1 tsp. salt and 1 c. hot water. Boil for 3 min. Pour over dumplings before baking. Bake at 350° for 45 min.

Peanut Butterscotch Drops

1 pkg. butterscotch bits, ¼ c. peanut butter, 2½ c. cornflakes. Melt chips in top of a double boiler, add peanut butter and cornflakes. Mix together, then drop by spoonful on greased wax paper and let cool. (This is so easy, the kids could help.)

Hans Waschtlin

Leftover pie dough. Roll out thin. Spread with applebutter. Roll up like jelly roll and cut in ½" rolls. Lay them in a pie pan with cut side down and bake. Makes a good treat for the children.

Graham Goodies

4 c. graham flour	2 c. white flour
1 c. brown sugar	1 c. butter or lard
1 tsp. soda	1 tsp. salt
1 heaping tsp. baking powder	1 c. sweet milk

Roll thin, bake at 475°.

Blondies

1 c. self-rising flour	1 c. oatmeal
(or 1 c. flour,	2 eggs
½ tsp. salt and	1 tsp. lemon extract (or lemon juice)
1 tsp. baking	1 tsp. vanilla
powder)	⅔ c. cooking oil
1⅓ c. light brown sugar	

Mix all ingredients in medium-sized bowl. Spread into a 9" x 9" pan. Bake at 350° for 30 min. Cut into 36 squares.

Recipe For Old Age

When my hair is thin and silvered;
and my time of toil is through;
When I've many years behind me,
and ahead of me a few:
I shall want to sit, I reckon,
sort of dreaming in the sun,
And recall the roads I've traveled
and the many things I've done.
I hope there'll be no picture
that I'll hate to look upon,
When the time to paint it better
or to wipe it out is gone.
I hope there'll be no vision
of a hasty word I've said
That has left a trail of sorrow,
like a whip welt sore and red.
And I hope my old-age dreaming
will bring back no bitter scene
Of a time when I was selfish,
or a time when I was mean.
When I'm getting old and feeble,
and I'm far along life's way,
I don't want to sit regretting
any bygone yesterday.
I am painting now the picture
that I'll want someday to see;
I am filling in a canvas
that will soon come back to me.
Though nothing great is on it,
and though nothing there is fine,
I shall want to look it over
when I'm old and call it mine.
So I do not dare to leave it
while the paint is warm and wet,
With a single thing upon it
that I later will regret.

- Author Unknown

Beverages, Jellies, and Miscellaneous

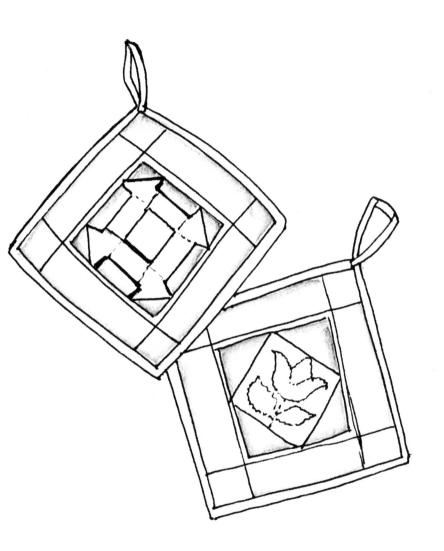

Ruby Jelly

3 med. raw diced beets, cover with water and boil 20-30 min. until well bled. Strain 3 c. juice. Add: 1 pkg. Certo crystals (or pectin), 3 T. lemon juice. Bring to hard boil, add 4 c. white sugar and boil hard for 4-5 min. Cool and seal. If you add 1 pkg. grape jello) to the above you get grape jelly. This jelly is good on toast.

Orpha's Apple Butter

5 gal. apples
1 tsp. cinnamon
1 c. vinegar

10 lb. sugar
¼ tsp. cloves

Cut up apples (unpeeled) in quarters; put apples, sugar and spices in large cooker. Cover tightly and place over low or simmer overnight. Do not lift lid; in morning add 1 c. vinegar, simmer 6 hr. more over low heat without removing lid. Then put through victoria strainer or food mill. May be used for snitz pies, putting in desired flavor.

Glorified Apple Butter

1 qt. white karo
1 qt. applesauce

1 c. white sugar

Cook this to heavy jam, then add:

1 pt. apple butter from store   ½ box strawberry jello

Zucchini Butter
"A mock apple butter"

4 c. cooked and blended
    zucchini
    (remove seeds)
4 T. vinegar
2 c. sugar

1 tsp. lemon juice
1 tsp. cinnamon
⅛ tsp. allspice
½ c. red hots candy (if desired)

Put in crockpot or in oven and cook to the desired thickness. We like this better than apple butter and it's cheaper.

Flower Honey

5 lb. white sugar   1½-2 c. water

Boil till clear.

Add alum size of a big cherry. Boil 2 min. Set back on stove, then put in:

8 good smelling pink roses
10 red clover blossoms
20 white clover blossoms

Press down in syrup with spoon. Let stand 10 min. Strain, then cool. This is very good.

Pineapple Jelly

6 c. sugar   1 c. water

Boil 10 min.
Add 3 c. crushed pineapples; boil 5 min.
Add 1 tsp. alum. Put in jars.

Tomato Cocktail

4 qt. tomatoes   ½ bunch celery
2 med. onions   16 whole cloves, put in a bag
1 green pepper   (remove when cooked)

Cook and put through sieve.

Add: 4 T. sugar, 4 T. lemon juice, 2 T. salt, ½ tsp. pepper, 4 T. vinegar. Cook the above 15 min. and seal.

Seasoning for Tomato Juice

½ c. celery salt   3 T. sugar
½ c. onion salt   2 T. pepper
2 T. garlic salt   1 c. table salt

Mix all together and add 1 level tsp. to each qt. of tomato juice when canning. I also use this to can vegetable soup.

Grape Juice

10 lb. grapes
3 lb. sugar

2 c. water

Wash grapes, add water and cook until soft. Strain through a cloth. Add sugar and bring to boil. Ladle into jars and seal.

Spiced Cider

6 c. sweet cider
½ tsp. grated lemon rind

3 sticks cinnamon
½ tsp. grated orange rind

Dandelion Jelly

In the early morning, pick 1 qt. of blossoms without any of the stems attached. Wash them. Now boil blossoms with qt. of water for 3 min. Drain off 3 c. liquid, discard blossoms. Add 1 pkg. of Sure-Jell, 1 tsp. of lemon or orange extract and 4½ c. sugar. Boil about 3 min., then skim off top. Put in jars and seal. Its taste resembles honey. Good on any bread.

Mock Raspberry Jelly

5 c. ground green tomatoes
4 c. sugar

Bring to a rolling boil and boil for 20 min. Keep stirring. Turn off heat. Add 6 oz. box Jello brand red raspberry jello. Stir till dissolved and put in jars. Simply delicious. Tastes like the real thing.

Red Beet Jelly

6 c. of juice from cooked beets (strained)
2 pkg. of Sure-Jell
8 c. sugar
½ c. lemon juice
2 - 6 oz. pkg. of red raspberry jello

Heat beet juice, Sure-Jell and lemon juice to a boil. Add sugar and jello. Bring to boil for 5 min. Seal in jars or glasses.

Orange-Rhubarb Drink

Cook 12 c. rhubarb in 3 c. water. Pour into a cloth bag to drip. To the juice add 4 c. sugar and 1 pkg. orange-flavored Kool-Aid. This concentrate can be canned. Add water until it is desired for a refreshing drink. Approx. 3 gal. to the total above concentrate. We also like to mix pineapple juice to it when opening a can of concentrate.

Pineapple Rhubarb Drink

3 c. pineapple juice   1½ c. sugar
3 c. rhubarb scant   4 c. water

Cook these ingredients together for 5 min. and strain in sieve. Add juice of 1 lemon and 1¼ c. frozen orange juice. Add gingerale and water to suit taste.

Zippy Rootbeer

2 c. white sugar   2 T. or more rootbeer
½ tsp. yeast   3 raisins

Put all in a gallon jug and fill with warm water. Set out in sun for 1 day and cool.

Hot Chocolate Mix

8 c. instant milk   1½ c. sugar
8 oz. creamer   ¾ c. baking soda
1 lb. Nestle's Quick cocoa

Mix and sift in large bowl. Store in dry place.
Use ½ c. of mix for 1 c. hot water.

Quick Rootbeer

2 c. white sugar   1 T. rootbeer extract
1 tsp. yeast

Melt sugar with hot water and pour in gallon jug. Put in water to fill till lukewarm. Add extract and yeast.
Let set in warm sun for ½ day, then turn cap loose and put in cold place.
Ready to drink the next day.

Lemonade

3 lemons, sliced
Mash with 2 c. sugar.
Mix well then let set for ½ hr. Then add 1 gal. water.

Cappuccino Drink Mix

1 c. hot chocolate mix
½ c. sugar

1 c. non-dairy creamer (French Vanilla)
¼ c. instant coffee

Mix and store in a container. Mix this mixture with boiling water to suit your taste.

Refreshing Punch

1 lg. can frozen orange
1 lg. can frozen lemon

1 qt. box orange sherbert
2 bottles gingerale

Beat first three ingredients, then add gingerale.

V-8 Juice

8 qt. of tomatoes, chopped (Simmer until soft, put through a sieve and set aside.)

2 c. tomato juice
2 lg. onions
1¼ c. diced celery
    and leaves
1½ tsp. salt
½ tsp. pepper

1 bell pepper (chopped)
2 tsp. dry basil
4 bay leaves
3 tsp. sugar
2 tsp. Worcestershire sauce

Boil together, then pick out bay leaves, put through sieve. Add ¾ c. white vinegar. Add remaining juice and boil, salt for taste.

Party Punch

3 lg. cans frozen
    orange juice
4 qt. 7-Up

2 lg. cans frozen lemonade
2 - 1 qt. cans pineapple juice
½ c. sugar (optional)

Add water as directed in frozen juices. Add 7-Up and ice. Serves 100.

Tea Concentrate

4 c. water   2 c. tightly packed fresh tea leaves
2 c. sugar

Boil water and sugar together 5 min. Add tea leaves and cover. Let set 6 hr. or overnight. Strain. Use 1 c. concentrate to 2 qt. water. Keeps in refrigerator a while or can be frozen. Tastes like fresh tea.

Cocoa Mix

4 lb. powdered milk   2 lb. Nestle's Quik
1 can creamorea
    (coffee cream)

Mix and store in container. For a hot drink, mix 1 T. mix to 1 c. hot water.

Egg Nog

1 c. milk   ½ tsp. vanilla
1 egg   1 T. sugar
nutmeg

Beat and chill.

Friendship Tea

9 oz. Tang (sm. jar)   ¾ oz. Lipton iced tea
12 oz. Wylers Presweetened   2 c. sugar
    Lemonade mix   2 tsp. cinnamon

Mix well and put in tight container. Put 2 heaping tsp. in cup, add hot water or cold water.

Fried Cornmeal Mush

3 c. yellow cornmeal   2 qt. boiling water
1 tsp. salt   ½ c. white flour

Bring water to a boil. Sift together cornmeal, salt and flour. Slowly add dry ingredients to boiling water, stirring constantly to prevent lump. Cook till done, pour into flat pans to mold. Let stand overnight. Cut slices ¼" thick and fry on both sides till golden brown. Delicious with tomato gravy, hot maple syrup or apple butter.

Sandwich Spread

First Part:

6 lg. green tomatoes	6 red peppers
6 onions	6 green peppers

Grind through a food chopper. Sprinkle with a handful of salt and let set 2 hr. Drain 30 min. Then pour 2 pt. vinegar over this and cook 15 min.

Second Part:

1 c. flour	1 tsp. turmeric
1 pt. mustard	1 pt. vinegar
5 c. sugar	

Mix this together and stir in first part like for any thickening and cook 15 min. Put in jars and seal. May be sealed with paraffin.

Fried Eggplant

2 med.-sized eggplants	2 eggs
1 tsp. salt	1 c. cracker crumbs
a little pepper	

Pare eggplant and slice ¼" thick. Beat eggs, salt and pepper together. Dip eggplants in egg mixture and roll in cracker crumbs. Fry in hot fat until golden brown on both sides. Tastes a lot like fish!

Drawing Salve

½ lb. white Rosin	4 oz. gum camphor
½ lb. bees wax	6 oz. soft soap (dish wash soap)
½ lb. mutton tallow or sheep lard	

Put first three ingredients in a pan to dissolve, add rest while cooling. Cut camphor fine before putting it in jars. Use for a drawing salve.

Roach Remedy

1 c. flour   16 oz. boric acid
1 sm. chopped onion   ¼ c. shortening or oil

Enough water to form a stiff dough. Shape into sm. balls and place where you think roaches hide, etc. Make sure no children or pets get these, as they are poisonous.

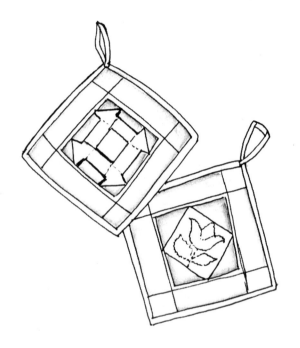